THE ALPS

THE ALPS

STEPHEN LEE

B.T. Batsford Ltd

To Carole

Printed in Great Britain by
Butler and Tanner, Frome, Somerset

ISBN 0 7134 5997 2

Acknowledgements

Extract taken from *The Lord of the Rings*, by
J.R.R. Tolkein, reproduced by kind permission of
Unwin Hyman Ltd. © Unwin Hyman Ltd.
Extract from *Big Yellow Taxi*, by Joni Mitchell,
reproduced by kind permission of Warner Chappell
Music Ltd. © Warner Chappell Music.
Extract taken from *Mont Blanc to Everest*, by
Guston Rebuffat, reproduced by kind permission of
Thames and Hudson. ©Thames and Hudson.

*Frontispiece. Ski mountaineer, Bernese Oberland
and the Matterhorn on the far central horizon.*

*Photographs throughout this book are by the
author*

Contents

List of Black and White Illustrations

List of Colour Plates

(between pages 80 and 81)

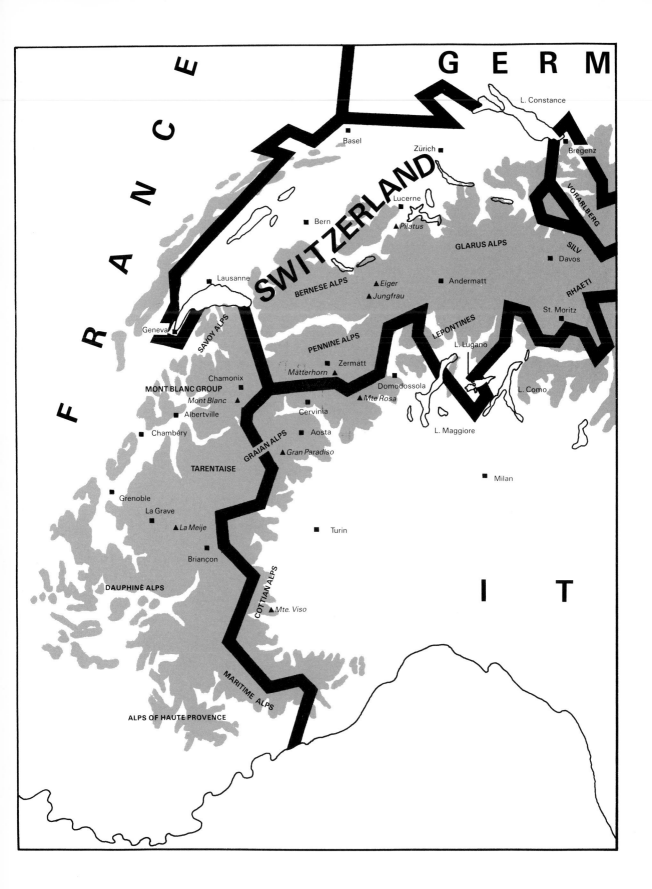

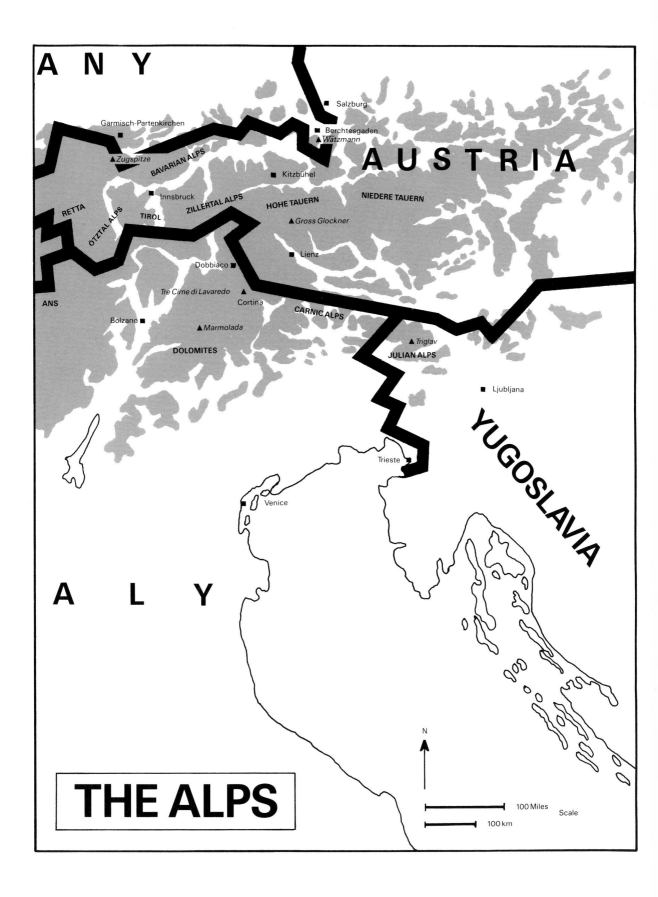

ANY

AUSTRIA

■ Salzburg

■ Garmisch-Partenkirchen
■ Berchtesgaden
▲ *Watzmann*

▲ *Zugspitze*

BAVARIAN ALPS

■ Kitzbühel

NIEDERE TAUERN

RETTA

■ Innsbruck

ZILLERTAL ALPS

HOHE TAUERN

TIROL

ÖTZTAL ALPS

▲ *Gross Glockner*

■ Lienz

ANS

Dobbiaco ■

Tre Cime di Lavaredo ▲
Cortina ■

CARNIC ALPS

■ Bolzano

▲ *Marmolada*

▲ *Triglav*

JULIAN ALPS

DOLOMITES

■ Ljubljana

YUGOSLAVIA

■ Trieste

ALY

■ Venice

N

THE ALPS

100 Miles

100 km

Scale

CHAPTER ONE

Introduction

The great mountains [the Himalayas] give their flashes of beauty; Makalu is indescribably impressive; but on the whole they are disappointing and infinitely less beautiful than the Alps.

— Mallory, written at the end of his first visit to Everest.

The 650 miles (1000 km) of the Alps may be a unit in the public mind, yet the Alps comprise some 20 distinct massifs which span very different countries – France, Switzerland, Italy, Germany, Austria and Yugoslavia. Each of these 20 massifs, or six countries, would merit a book in itself and still leave the reader hungry for more. The unifying factor, in historical terms at least, is that traditionally inhabitants would take their animals up to summer pastures ('alps') below the snow-line. Now this is mostly done by truck rather than by the shepherd.

An obvious, perhaps pedestrian, approach to such a well-trodden subject would be to tackle the Alps massif by massif. This would result in yet another book on the Alps whose regional sections would surely be unsatisfactory, given the enormous scope of the undertaking.

The answer is to be selective, and to examine the component parts which really do unify the Alps as a mountain range, both from the viewpoint of the inhabitants, and the visitors. What are these common factors? First one looks at 'alps'. Originally these were no more than summer mountain pastures. In many areas, bringing in the harvest is no easier today than it

was 100 years ago. And this is the key to these tenuously linked massifs. They are named after inaccessible pastures in a hard but rewarding environment which has shaped the people and the way we see them. These then are the real unities; the people, their customs, their food and gastronomy, their harvests, their festivals, their flowers and birds, their wines, their buildings, and their livelihoods.

And the latter, livelihood, is the link between the inhabitants and us, the travellers. Tourism – the desire to explore, to photograph, to walk, to climb, to ski, to eat and drink the produce of another land, seeing scenery which is always spectacular, ever changing and mostly accessible – has joined our paths.

Visiting the Alps for pleasure is a comparatively new phenomenon. In Switzerland it goes back barely 200 years, and became of economic significance only some 100 years ago. Formerly, because of population pressures, Swiss Alpine districts had to export their populations – to find work in the lowlands, abroad as mercenaries, or as permanent exiles. Now there is generally enough work for everyone, with much of the cheap basic labour coming from outside.

Only recently has the concept of holiday travel become widely accepted, not just for physical well-being, but also for resting the mind. The Alps, described by Leslie Stephen in 1871 as the 'playground of Europe', were regarded as far from this by their medieval neighbours. Akin to an acceptance of the Alps was also the acceptance of the fact of vacation, a break from the everyday routine of work. The American judge Brandeis correctly pointed out that he could easily get through 12 months' work in 11 months, but not in 12 months. That understood, the only question was what to do with one's leisure. Travel became a major recreation in itself. The Alps have been much written about, much visited, photographed and painted, ravaged, so press and TV reports would tell us, to the point that there is little more pleasure to be had of them. But this is not the case.

1. The Watzmann, Berchtesgaden, Germany.

Access, accommodation and tourism are well developed. This means that the average person who has no great desire to risk his life hanging from a rock face miles from the valley floor can still get to the heart of the Alps by car, train, and cablecar with no more effort than reaching for his wallet.

For the others to whom such cheque-book adventure is anathema, there are still thousands of square miles which, while not unmapped, are still available for the personal challenge. Technology may make the mountains ever easier to conquer, but wind, avalanche and human error still dog our footsteps as they did in the days when Balmat and Paccard first ascended Mont Blanc. Danger and adventure are still the by-words of the mountains.

The popularity of major and minor peaks has meant that many mountains are now indistinguishable from the history of men and women who tried, failed and succeeded on them. The Dolomites thus took their name, the Whymper couloir, the Bonnatti pillar, the 'American Direct' on the Drus. Men have named and mapped and strutted on their summits, but the mountains remain unmoved.

A new look at the Alps
First came the rock, then the animals and then man. This book begins with the historical and geographical aspects of the range. The text moves on to specific chapters designed for the reader with a particular interest.

2. Albergo, Ascona, Switzerland.

The Alpine Range (chapter 2) deals with the physical features of the Alps as a geographical unity, wherever this is possible. We look at how the Alps were formed, the physical relationship between the Alpine countries, the formation of glaciers and other physical phenomena. We also point the traveller at various places where the action of the years and erosion has left a living museum of how the Alps were formed.

History and Exploration of the Alps (chapter 3) shows how the Alps were opened up by man, and, surprisingly, how recently this happened. The fear of God and superstition plagued early

3. Mountain Hut, Haute Route, France.

explorations. Due to lack of knowledge and suitable equipment, the result was invariably an epic and exaggerated tale of mountain dangers. We examine the Alps as a barrier from the time of Hannibal to Napoleon and the present day; the Alps as a barrier in war; and the hostilities and alliances of Alpine countries from early times to the present. Some explored because of necessity, as fugitives or in search of grazing for their herds, but the concept of a voluntary visit to the domain of the chamois has only existed for a couple of centuries.

Alpine People (chapter 4) covers traditional Alpine occupations: for example, the daily life of a shepherd or mountain guide, Alpine customs, architecture, contacts with the outside world, tourism and its effects on traditional Alpine life.

The Natural Life of the Alps (chapter 5) takes a look at the flora and fauna of the Alpine chain, with details of the natural habitats, animals, birds and flowers which are most likely to be encountered, where the more accessible can be seen, as well as Alpine zoos and gardens. 'The politics of pollution' discusses the very great pressure put on the Alps by tourism and industry, while introducing the concept of National Parks and areas of preservation.

Visiting the Alps (chapter 6) deals with the bare bones of an Alpine journey, whether the traveller starts from the USA, the British Isles, or from mainland Europe. The seasons and their likely effect on the visitor are discussed, when and how to go, and how to travel around the Alps. The 'Alps at a glance' is a detailed factual gazette on travel in each Alpine country.

Photography in the Alps (chapter 7) is a guide to the best techniques, places and seasons to practise the noble art of landscape photography. Reference is made to the early Alpine painters and photographers, and to their effect on research, documentation and exploration. Detailed technical advice on mountain photography both above and below the snow line is given.

The Alps by Train (chapter 8) is a guide to the many beautiful parts of the Alps which are accessible by train, describing routes into the Alps as well as the great mountain train trips within the Alps – the Glacier Express, the Jungfraujoch railway and points of interest along the way. We also examine rail travel options within each country.

The Alps by Car (chapter 9) looks at the practicalities of Alpine motoring, hiring a car, driving to and within the Alps, seasonal closures of passes, motoring in winter conditions. 'Classic' itineraries in each country are offered to the motorist.

Alpine Food and Wine (chapter 10) The traveller might be encouraged to take a gastronomic tour of the Alps. Perhaps he might like to visit the Alpes Vaudoises where he could meet the cheese-makers of this area; or try the cured ham of the Grisons, or the pasta of the Dolomites. He might encounter a wine-grower of the Rhône valley who discusses the problems of reaping a good harvest so close to the snow line. But this same vintner may welcome the snow, for in the winter he may be a ski instructor in a low-altitude ski resort with a short season. We learn about the traditional food of the Alps.

Walking in the Alps (chapter 11) The walker, now well fuelled, might like to undertake some of the classic walks of Europe. The tour of Mont Blanc is a fabulous high-altitude route in sight of Europe's highest summit. The Alte Vie of the Aosta valley give the Italian perspective. The Alpine Pass Route is struggling for deserved recognition. Pointers on equipment and advice for the beginner are given.

Climbing in the Alps (chapter 12) selects some of the classic Alpine peaks, with their histories and an outline of how they are best approached today. The chapter includes the history of some of the great mountaineering climbs, e.g. Mont Blanc, the Eiger, the Matterhorn, as well as advice for the beginner.

Skiing in the Alps (chapter 13) deals in outline with the history of recreational skiing, which has only just celebrated its centenary. Also discussed are ski mountaineering and cross-country skiing, by which skiers can reach parts of the Alps which are inaccessible by chairlift. The World Cup ski circuit and new wave skiiing are examined too. The chapter closes with a selection of two or three main resorts in each Alpine country.

Mountain Dangers (chapter 14) dispels some of the myths and legends about avalanches, altitude sickness, wind chill, snow blindness, and crevasses, which will be of interest to all Alpinists, armchair or in the flesh.

More Alpine Sports (chapter 15) goes into alternative Alpine sports for those in search of a thrill – hang-gliding, parapente, ballooning, rafting, mountain biking, riding, the Cresta run and the four-man bob.

4. Ski Touring, Bernese Oberland, Switzerland.

Please note:

In *Über den Granit* (1784), two years before Mont Blanc was conquered, no less an authority than Goethe declared that it was an impossible task for a mere writer to attempt to describe the immensity of the Alps. It was better by far, he said, to attempt to analyze them.

By 1800 visitors were turning out so many Alpine travelogues that the market was flooded and even contemporary holiday-makers were unable to keep up with the flow of Alpine ink. Think where we stand in 1991!

Two centuries on, not even Scheuchzer would claim to have written a definitive book on anything Alpine, except perhaps on Alpine dragons.

I think I will listen to Goethe. Rather than attempt to describe the immensity of the Alps, I will attempt to analyze them. This is not designed to be a comprehensive place-by-place guide to every part of the Alps. Its aim is to encourage English-speaking visitors throughout the world to visit, and to give some pointers so they can make their own decisions on Alpine travel. A book which seeks to inform an Alpine visitor about every facet of the Alpine holiday would need to run to a couple of dozen volumes. This book will show the reader how best to visit the Alps and where to find more detailed information, should it be required.

5. *Richardière, Vercors, France.*

CHAPTER TWO

The Alpine Range

Eastward the . . . downs rose, ridge behind ridge into the morning, and
vanished out of eyesight into a guess; it was no more than a guess of blue and
a remote white glimmer blending with the hem of the sky, but it spoke to
them, out of memory and old tales, of the high and distant mountains.

— J.R.R. Tolkein, *Lord of the Rings.*

The Alpine chain is an arc of some 650 miles (1000 km) by 100 (160 km) or so miles wide. On a perfect day you might see the spectre of the first peaks of the Maritime Alps from the seashore at Nice, while 650 or so miles to the east the Alpine arc dissipates into the plains of Austria and to the sea near Trieste. Many peaks exceed 4000 m (13,000 ft), innumerable peaks 3000 m (10,000 ft).

Defining the Alps can be a tricky business. The satellite pictures seen on weather maps make clear the half-moon shape stretching almost from the Mediterranean to the Adriatic, but on the ground it is harder to see the link. Martin Conway had less difficulty with this concept when he walked the Alps from end to end in 1894, but for others the existence of a number of different chains may be a hindrance to understanding the unity.

Some would exclude the Dolomites, geologically and geographically. Others would not automatically include the Bavarian Alps of Germany, which might however take great exception to being left out of an Alpine book. After all, it is highly fashionable and profitable to

be part of the Alps, with all that this implies for modern tourism. There may be many places, plains and valleys between ranges, where the map 'goes green' (and therefore snowless) and one might think that we have run out of Alps. But the unifying factor is the 'alp', the high-altitude pasture where shepherds take their animals in summer when the winter snows have receded. It is the traditional habits of the people as much as fine geographical distinctions between individual ranges which makes a mountain Alpine.

Because the Alps were formed, in simple terms, by the crushing pressure of two continents meeting from north and south, many of the some 20 individual massifs are roughly aspected east to west.

To those of us who are not geologists, but who are curious as to how this mighty chain was formed, Alpine literature is often a source of great disappointment. Words like *morainic nunatak*, *pingoes* and *cryocongeliturbate* do not exactly trip off the tongue. Yet these and other equally abstruse phrases pepper Alpine literature with confusion. Mark Twain gets closer to the spirit of simplicity with his tight but clear description of Switzerland as 'simply a large, humpy, solid rock, with a thick skin of grass stretched over it'.

Many millions of years ago, the Alps, and most of Europe for that matter, were covered by the sea. The solid crust of the sea floor consisted of sedimentary rock which was formed of the sediment of marine creatures, shells etc., which accumulated over millions of years. Common types of sedimentary rock are chalk and limestone. These formed on top of crystalline rock, such as granite, itself solidified from molten rock.

The continents met, agreed to differ, reared up and folded. They were forced out of the sea to form the land mass and the Alps. Three main folds concern us; a central east–west fold, a western and an eastern fold running roughly north–south.

The moment these surprised rocks lifted their heads out of the sea, the forces of erosion began to work on them. First to go was the sedimentary rock, often exposing crystalline rock beneath. Thus the main chain, the Monte Rosa, the Bernina and the Hohe Tauern are mostly composed of crystallised rock.

Other folds to the north and south also rose, but not so high. We now see the limestone Alps of the North Tirol, Salzburg and the Bernese Oberland, and the Dolomites and Julian Alps to the south. The highest of these sedimentary rocks is the Eiger.

The east–west folds would sprout watersheds to the north and south. Rivers would, in turn, meet lesser folds and have to turn east or west. Hence the Rhône valley. This would have remained remarkably simple had the meeting of the continental plates been left to this, but a second fold, north–north–east to south–south–west, took place. In places like the Bernese Oberland, the Mont Blanc Chain and parts of the Dauphiné, summits pushed up through sedimentary strata. The summit of that minor but famous peak, the Rigi, just 2000 m high, has

pebbly sedimentary rocks from a river delta. This gives some idea of the immensity of the earth's upheaval. The basic shaping of the Alps has been, and still is, immensely slow work. For the moment we are more concerned with the factors which can be observed today – the snow cover, glaciation, avalanches.

As soon as the glaciers began to retreat some 16,000 to 20,000 years ago, occasional nomads began to explore above the snow line. The tree-line became established at around 2000 m (6500 ft) largely where it is today, albeit with considerable local variation.

EROSION

Reading about the power of glaciers, one might think that they alone are the great eroding power of the Alps. But water does the job far more quickly, and even wind has its fair share of success over softer rock. Heat and cold are the other factors. Although the Alps are still pushing ever upward at about $\frac{1}{8}$ in (2 mm) a year, they are being eroded by about 1 mm a year. Crystalline rock in the higher major folds erodes more slowly than sedimentary rock, often seen in lesser folds in the pre-Alps. Some of the most unusual examples of erosion are found in various parts of the Alps in the form of earth pyramids at Euseigne, in Switzerland's Valais region, the Ritten in the Dolomites near Bolzano, and the Casse Deserte near the Col D'Izouard in the French Dauphiné.

THE LIFE OF A GLACIER

Eighty per cent of the world's fresh water is deposited in ice and snow; 97 per cent of this is in Greenland and Antarctica. The snows and glaciers of the Alps represent only a tiny percentage of this, yet there is plenty to go round.

Twenty million years ago, much of Europe was covered by a tropical sea. Where we now ski on the Lac des Vaux, voracious sharks patrolled the muddy waters. Instead of pines and chamois,

palm and rubber tree forests were prowled by mastodons, rhinoceri and flamingos. In those days, holiday companies offering a snow guarantee would have gone out of business very quickly indeed.

Then, some three million years ago, we had an

6. *Earth pyramids, Ritten, South Tirol.*

ice age, with the average temperature about 15°C (60°F) colder than it is today. Since then glaciers have been steadily retreating, with the exception of a mini ice age between AD 1600 and 1850.

Today we think of glaciers as large lumps of slow-moving ice conveniently placed near ski resorts for summer skiing, useless for anything else. Yet glaciers are a mine of information about the earth's past, recent and distant. By taking core samples out of the ice, major volcanic eruptions (Krakatoa 1883) or sandstorms from the Sahara hundreds or thousands of years ago can be dated quite accurately.

Glaciers are also an invaluable method of monitoring what man is doing to his environment. Glaciologists can accurately pinpoint evidence of the first deforestations and pollution, the first nuclear testing (1953) and the effects of permeation of the ozone layer. Some of the work of glaciologists concerns the forecasting of ice avalanches falling from glaciers, which can have catastrophic effects on mountain villages.

Within living memory, Alpine dwellers hacked off large lumps of ice for refrigeration, or kept their milk in crevasses.

Formation of glaciers

Glaciers are born in the gullies around mountain peaks. Layer upon layer of snow deposited over time causes pressure which turns loose snow into 'firn' snow. It will take about 20 ft (6 m) of powder snow to make 2 ft (60 cm) of firn snow. More pressure and melting snow filling in the cavities turns firn snow into firn ice and eventually into glacier ice. The whole process from snow fall to glacier ice takes about five years.

Types of glacier

Paulke and Dumler, in *Hazards in Mountaineering*, classified glaciers as follows. Most of the great glaciers of the Alps are valley glaciers. Cirque or corrie glaciers are found above the snow line, for example on the east face of the Watzmann near Berchtesgaden in Germany. Plateau glaciers are situated on tablelands, for example the Übergossene Alm in the Berchtesgaden Alps. Gorge glaciers are usually fed by avalanches in sunless gorges and valley floors – the Taconnaz Glacier in the Mont Blanc range.

Hanging glaciers cling to steep faces lying above cliffs such as at Titlis, Engelberg. Brittle rotten ice forms on glaciers during the summer melt of snow and firn ice. Percolated water covers the faces with a smooth hard veneer and fills up the cracks. Glazed ice ('verglas') also comes from melt-water and is usually found in mid-summer or autumn. Such completely smooth verglas can make any ascent or ski descent very dangerous.

Why glaciers advance or recede

Obviously the growth rate of glaciers depends on the amount of snow which falls each winter, but more important still is whether there is also snow in summer, and whether summer is cold or warm. Snow melts equally quickly whether it is on a glacier or on rock. The ideal conditions for glacial growth are warm winters and cool summers. Warm air holds more moisture and therefore there will be heavier snowfalls than when it is very cold. A cooler than average summer gives the glacier a double growth period in any given year.

The next ice age?

In the last 100 years, glaciers have been gradually retreating, but the next ice age is not as far away as you might think. We are getting cooler summers as the sun has to penetrate an increasingly polluted atmosphere. Also the atmosphere (consisting of water vapour and ozone) has a 'greenhouse effect' holding the earth's heat in, keeping the average temperature to around 15°C (60°F). Without this greenhouse effect the average temperature would be about −20°C (−4°F). The holes which we are beginning to notice in the ozone layer are not just scientific curiosities – they could lead to real problems. It would only take a drop in average temperature of a couple of degrees C before we are slowly moving towards another ice age.

Features on the surface of a glacier

Moraines consist of debris fallen from rock slopes and carried down by the glacier. Loose lateral moraines are at the side of a glacier. Medial moraines are found at the confluence of glaciers. Terminal moraines are situated at the

7. Drus, Mer de Glace, France.

foot of a glacier. Crevasses are usually visible on bare glaciers, which extend from the foot to the snowline. Ropes should be carried both on bare glaciers and on snow-covered glaciers, particularly when snow bridges are not consolidated.

Crevasses occur when the ice cracks in sympathy with the ground shape, either on corners or more particularly when the ground drops over a concave slope. Firn ice is more brittle than glacier ice and more prone to crevasses. Crevasses change, close up or widen from year to year. Bergschrunds occur when the more solid ice of the glacier breaks away from the less stable layer of ice on the walls, which is usually frozen to the bottom.

Crevasses can be spotted by a slight sinking of the snow cover, by dark fracture lines on the snow surface, or in summer, by white snow indicating bridges as opposed to ice or firn which will be blue-green. Those travelling over crevassed terrain should be equipped for and practised at crevasse rescue.

Other notable features of glaciers are icefalls, which are formed as transverse crevasses when the surface of the glacier is broken up into towers (seracs). These are extremely dangerous. Also dangerous are glacier tables, which are large isolated slab-like rocks. The melting away of the ice beneath can leave huge rocks resting on a support of ice.

How fast do glaciers move?

Different glaciers flow at different speeds. These can be as slow as 10 ft (3 m) a year, e.g. the Blaueis glacier in the Hochkalter range. Or they travel as fast as the Aletsch glacier in the Bernese Oberland (some 10 miles (16 km) long) which moves at up to 100 yds (90 m) per annum. The speed is related to the angle of the terrain beneath the glacier as well as its size. In the Chamonix area the 4-mile (7-km) Glacier des Bossons is in places at an angle of 50 degrees and advances at about 150 yds (135 m) per annum. By comparison the almost flat Mer de Glace, round the corner on the skiable Vallée Blanche, travels at about 80 yds (70 m) per annum.

Glacier speeds are quite predictable. In 1820 three Chamonix mountain guides were swept by an avalanche into a crevasse on the Grand Plateau. The English geologist J.D. Forbes made the macabre prediction that in 35–40 years their bodies would emerge at the foot of the glacier. Sure enough, 41 years later, the Glacier des Bossons surrendered their bodies.

The destructive power of glaciers

Dangers to mountaineers and skiers may be obvious, but glaciers can cause immense catastrophes to people living in the valleys below. These may be due to the breaking away of entire sections of glaciers, massive avalanches of ice and snow, or flooding caused by the outburst of a glacier-dammed lake. In 1595 such a lake outburst killed 160 in Gietro in Switzerland, and as recently as August 1965 an ice avalanche killed 88 in Allalin.

In an ice avalanche in 1895 at Altels, 4.5 million cubic metres (5 million cubic yds) of ice broke away in a slab 600 yds (550 m) long and 45 yds (40 m) thick. Ice avalanches have a habit of recurring since the dangerous configurations of ice and snow will sooner or later be repeated. Today, ice avalanches are monitored and lakes known to be dangerous are dammed and routinely drained. The Swiss, not surprisingly, have developed an expertise in this field. They monitor the minutest changes in the position of ice-falls with aerial photography and lasers which are accurate to $\frac{1}{8}$ in (2 mm).

Glaciers for piste-skiers

Of course glaciers as skiers know them are generally at their safest in winter when there is a thick and well consolidated snow cover. Many glaciers are accessible to the skier for the price of a lift ticket. Others are the domain only of the ski mountaineer or mountaineer.

Glacier watching

The non-skiing or non-climbing glacier watcher can have a good look at glaciers for the price of a rail ticket by visiting Montenvers in the Chamo-

8. Crevasses, Glacier des Bossons, Chamonix.

nix valley of France, or the Jungfraujoch scientific station in Switzerland. The latter houses a fascinating exhibition on the history of glaciation and its relevance to man and animals. And through the window are fabulous views of the glacierland of the Bernese Oberland. By car, the Rhône glacier above Gletsch in Switzerland is easily accessible.

Glaciers are at their most spectacular in summer, when the crevasses are exposed. For those disinclined to venture to high altitudes, the Glacier Garden in Lucerne is worth a look.

Finally, for the armchair glacier watcher, the Swiss National Tourist Office have published an excellent book entitled *Switzerland and her Glaciers*. This is a history not only of glaciers but also of man's first attempts at Alpine exploration and systematic recording of glacial movement. In the early days painters (not photographers) were commissioned to record the glaciers, and the works of many famous early Alpine artists are beautifully reproduced here.

Over the last 150 years there has been a general pattern of retreat among the Alpine glaciers. A sustained advance or retreat of glaciers gives a good indication of trends in climate, perhaps more accurate than even measurement of temperature. The Grindelwald glacier in Switzerland has retreated about 1 mile (1.5 km) since 1850, suggesting warmer summers and winters with less snow.

CHAPTER THREE

History and Exploration of the Alps

Just and protective divinities find only flat surfaces acceptable.

— Archimedes.

'Everything in the Alps is frozen fast' wrote Silius Italicus (AD 20–100). This is not the way one would open a modern-day travel brochure. Men in Roman times did not venture into the mountains unless fleeing for their lives, under orders, or for gain or reward. Sport and recreation were strictly confined to the amphitheatre.

The establishment of Christianity in Western Europe necessitated many crossings of the Alps from north to south, but even then the preferred, but more expensive, route was by sea. Many Christians considered the crossing of the Alps as part of the penance, suggesting they might even prefer to take their chances in the amphitheatre than on the high Alpine passes.

Around the twelfth century, with the increase of trade, hospices were built at some of the major Alpine passes. The fact that increasing numbers of travellers were able to complete a crossing of the Alps and live to tell the tale gradually led to the Alps becoming less frightening. Word spread that it was possible to return from the snowline without necessarily being freeze-dried.

Later exploration came in the wake of colonialism and greed. These were at least some of the reasons behind the much-reported Hannibal expedition. But with the exception of one or two major gold-strikes, the quest for minerals and objects of value in the cold wet altitudes enriched few. Late in Roman times, herdsmen began to take their animals to better pastures above the Po valley, but almost without exception they returned with horror stories of malevolent mountain forces.

THE HANNIBAL DEBATE

Hannibal was one of the first to make news and war in the Alps. He was the first to cross the Alps with a sizeable army; some 30,000 foot soldiers and 37 elephants in 218 BC, from Spain. The crossing was probably made in late autumn when the first snow of winter had fallen.

Controversy still rages today as to the exact pass, mostly because of a number of differing translations of the work of Livy and Polybius. But we know he succeeded and much entertainment has been had in the guessing. As Mark Twain disrespectfully observes: 'The researches of many antiquarians have already thrown much darkness on the subject, and it is probable that if they continue, we shall soon know nothing at all'.

How could I venture a guess as to Hannibal's likely route after that? Suffice it to say that a few modern historians, notably Wolf Zeuner and

Gavin de Beer have become dedicated to the quest for the right pass taken by Hannibal after he had transported his elephants across the Rhône on rafts and turned east for Italy.

Candidates vary from the Montgenèvre, Mont Cenis, Little St Bernard, Col de Clapier, Col de Larche, Col de Mary and the Col de La Traversette. All of these, except for Col de Larche and Col de Mary, have been crossed by an elephant in the company of Wolf Zeuner. De Beer, using weather data and logistical analysis, came to the conclusion that the Col de la Traversette, high on the present French and Italian frontier ridge below Monte Viso, was the most likely pass.

Hannibal entered from the Durance valley, whence the easiest crossing would have been over the comparatively easy Col de Montgenèvre, past modern-day Briançon. The Traversette route would have provided an apparently easy route past Mont Dauphin, becoming problematic later. It is also possible that the locals may have connived in leading him to choose La Traversette, hoping he would get into difficulties.

If he took this route, it was certainly harder than all the rest and a mistake. But once committed, he pressed on past Château Queyras, the 'bare rock' on which he may have bivouacked, and tramped on stubbornly through the early winter snows. Difficulties were enormous. It was another 1700 years before the road tunnel was to be built. Impassable rocks had to be split with fire and vinegar by the Carthaginians.

Hannibal's route will never really be finalized in the absence of archaeological evidence, but Wolf Zeuner cannot be blamed for lack of effort. Apart from feeding all available data into a computer, he went to Nepal and got to know six elephants on first-name terms, with the aim of bringing them back for a field test.

A feasibility study was made with a borrowed circus elephant and a lorry so the elephant did not become too tired. The lorry soon became jammed on a hairpin bend approaching the Petit Mont Cenis pass, and the elephant had to get out and walk. The elephant's performance was measured with radio telemetry. During this time it became clear that an elephant needs to acclimatize just like the rest of us. It needs gallons of water and for an animal with flat feet and no claws, it is remarkably sure-footed on steep ground. Apart from this we are not much the wiser about Hannibal.

THE ALPS AT WAR

In terms of losing Alps, Austria has had more than its fair share of bad luck. World Wars transferred half a million Austrians to Italy, renamed numerous Dolomite peaks, and shifted the Julian Alps from Austria into Yugoslavia.

The Swiss Gotthard pass and the Schoellenen gorge saw spirited action in the Napoleonic wars. The Russian general Suvorov, assisting the Austrians against the French, was chased around and over most of the passes in canton Uri. His exploits are commemorated by a monument above the gorge. Along the route was the famous 'Devil's bridge', so called because the Devil would only allow its construction if he could have the soul of the first living being to cross it. The Swiss sent him a goat. Years later, when the new bridge was built, they sent across another goat just in case.

Napoleon took the Grand St Bernard pass in an early and successful gamble against the Austrians in 1800. The crossing, unexpected by the Austrians, met with many technical difficulties, but allowed Napoleon to exact the peace treaties of 1800. Realizing the strategic importance of being able to cross the Alps quickly, he initiated a series of building works to make the Simplon and other passes suitable for transporting artillery. The foundations enabled rough tracks to become routes usable for heavy traffic which now form some of the major passes – Montgenèvre, Grand St Bernard and Simplon.

In the Dolomites, relics of the First World War are still to be seen. Whole mountain tops were blasted for strategic advantage, peaks were honeycombed with caves and ammunition dumps. A cross commemorates the many who died on Monte Piano, stray bullet shells still tell their tale, and a book names the dead at the Rifugio Bosi. Here the sad story of war was often one of almost individual man-to-man combat between families known to each other before hostilities began; the Italian Alpini, the Austrian Alpenjäger – one Alpine range, two nations and two sides.

Fierce fighting was also seen in the Julian Alps in the First World War. In the Second World War, the Maquis established centres of resistance in the Vercors plateau and the Julian Alps. Near Triglav in Yugoslavia stands a giant piton and carabiner as a memorial to the local partisans.

We hear of tactical stalemates in the French Alps with the Germans holding the top of a téléférique and the French the bottom. Situations such as this did little for the wintersports industry.

In the Second World War, Switzerland was able to maintain something of a semblance of neutrality, Hitler finding it far too convenient to keep the passes and tunnels open.

Today Alpine troops of all nationalities can be seen practising around and above the snowline. Let us hope there are no more lost Alps.

ATTITUDES TO THE ALPS

'There was something subduing in the influence of that silent and solemn and awful presence (the Jungfrau) . . . One had the sense of being under the brooding contemplation of a spirit, not an inert mass of rocks and ice – a spirit which had looked down, through the slow drift of the ages, upon a million vanished races of men, and judged them; and would judge a million more – and still be there, watching, unchanged and unchangeable after all life should be gone and the earth had become a vacant desolation.'
— Mark Twain, *A Tramp Abroad.*

In 1306 Petrarch climbed Mont Ventoux, was instantly homesick, became bored on the summit, and went home for self-analysis. Worse than this, he told everyone about it. It was to be 500 years before the Alps could even begin to clear their name.

Well into the seventeenth century, revulsion was the first reaction to the mountains. Man had had enough of nature. It was a damn nuisance. Cities were just becoming big and interesting enough to offer an alternative to the ceaseless shovelling of snow. Inhabitants of the Alps could barely eke a living from 45-degree pastures. Nor had the pressures of urban living become such that men wished to flee, as they do now, back to the mountains. They fled from them. The crossing of Alpine passes was frequently accomplished only at night or blindfolded, as if ignoring the view would somehow make the journey safer.

Superstition clung to the peaks. Mount Pilatus was believed to be haunted by the ghost of Pontius Pilate (though how he got there no one can say). Having been put out of bounds by the town council, the summit had to be exorcised by a priest in the 1530s. In 1690 the Bishop of Annecy exorcised the Glacier des Bossons in Chamonix. He must have been hot stuff, since the glacier was reported to have retreated a quarter of a mile (400 m) immediately.

Law and order was absent from many mountain valleys. The Bernese Oberland was said to crawl with bandits. Minorities like the Waldensians, persecuted into religious exile since the fourteenth century, wanted to remain secluded.

Monastic orders began to seek tranquillity in the mountains. Their tranquillity was often short-lived, as in the case of the monastery of Chartreuse, which soon had to build a hostel for visitors. Along the Mediterranean, the practice of transporting and selling snow as the essence of purity, a cure for various ailments, began to advertise the more positive, even if ill-founded, medicinal aspects of the Alps.

The sixteenth century saw an even greater

opening of the Alps. Men of learning flocked to the mountains to observe and record flora and fauna, and in their wake came the painters. Gradually the ideas of clean air, the fascination with glaciers, and the concept that the mountains were 'God's country' gained popularity. But not everyone was so keen to open the door to the Alps. Chamois hunters and crystal gatherers did little to assist the travellers, not wanting their hunting grounds to be known.

In 1721, Scheuchzer published a major work on the Alps, marred only by his insistence that Alpine dragons actually existed, since every local he met told him so. This slightly, if not terminally, tarnished his reputation. But he was in his time a strong advocate of the health-giving properties of the Alps, and the fact that they do have the ability to restore the tired spirit.

Goethe in 1775 was also captivated by the spirit of the Alps, but found the people to be circumscribed by the immensity of their landscape. 'You call the Swiss free? . . . in their medieval inward-looking towns? These poor devils clinging to their rocks and cliffs, when half the year the snow imprisons them in their hovels like marmots'.

Rousseau's novel *La Nouvelle Héloïse* did much to implant Switzerland and the Alps on the itinerary of the Grand Tour, by then well established as the ideal way to 'finish' the education of gentlemen of considerable means. Despite his lack of real Alpine knowlege (one suspects that Rousseau was a telescope Alpinist), this soft-core love story is set against an idealized Alpine background, extolling purity and simplicity to name but two Alpine virtues. One gets the impression that it is only possible to have such rarefied emotions in high places. Presumably the truism applies as much today as then – if you think you feel emotional about something, who can disagree?

Indignation throughout most of Europe followed the placing of the Swiss confederation under French protection. Suddenly freedom, democracy and independence were praised as the great virtues of the Swiss, whose institutions became the envy of Europe and were compared with ancient Greece.

Around this time the William Tell legend, a joint effort on the part of Schiller and Goethe, took hold of European imagination. Tell is seen as the archetypal Swiss hero, while the cantonal representatives are seen as 'wanting to live like their fathers in freedom in the mountains'.

Whether the Swiss were ever a nation of equal alpenstock-toting shepherds is a matter of debate. But that was how Europe saw them. And the Alps were by then firmly implanted on the non-alpine mind as God's country, a place of higher aspirations and even of attainable higher ground. Benefit could be had from each of these.

THE VERTICAL WORLD – CLIMBING AS EXPLORATION

The inhabitants of steep Alpine valleys would obviously have been skilled at moving around on high mountain territory for local journeys or everyday work. They must have developed a number of tricks of the trade which we now call mountaineering. Visitors acquired from the locals the knack of keeping warm by insulation, recognizing the worst places for avalanches, protecting their eyes from snow-blindness.

But climbing as we now understand it is done for pure sport, or, to borrow a much-used expression, 'because it is there'. This was said by Mallory, despite more recent attributions. The recorded ascent in 1492 of Mont Aiguille by the chamberlain of Charles VIII can hardly be described as climbing for the sake of it; the penalty for refusal might easily have been a court-martial.

Many of the earlier attempts on the peaks were in the name of science. The first real mountaineering ascent of the Alps' highest peak, Mont Blanc, was made by Balmat and Paccard in June 1786 at the instigation of the scientist Saussure. In the years that followed, cries were already heard about the hordes of 'touristes

inutiles' who were clogging up the slopes. Tourism began early in Chamonix.

And as literature and art had a revival of interest in things Alpine in the latter half of the eighteenth century, so the scientists began to visit and became the first Alpinists. In 1741 we have a record of Wyndham visiting from England and climbing the Montenvert in Chamonix. It was then not known that Mont Blanc was the highest peak in Europe and the Alps.

In fact the search for an accurate method of determining altitude was one of the earlier scientific reasons for Alpinism. Horace Benedict de Saussure in 1760 was more interested in the science of summitry, as was the landscape painter Marc-Theodore Burrit, arriving in Chamonix in 1766. The valley was filled with scientific visitors with barometers and apparatus to boil water and thereby determine altitude. A hundred years later, Mark Twain deals with this amusingly in *A Tramp Abroad*, where he ends

9. *Balmat and Saussure facing Mont Blanc.*

up boiling his altimeter and making altimeter soup.

Meanwhile, the age of guided climbing had arrived. Even the most famous, like Whymper, used the local guides. Later characters like Mummery pioneered a breed of impoverished amateur athletes, as capable as anyone of making the great ascents. Today sponsorship and personal challenge, not necessarily linked, are the watchwords of modern climbing.

The Swiss equivalent of de Saussure was a monk of Disentis, Placidus a Spescha, who was posted in 1781 from the Disentis monastery to the Lukmanier hospice, at an important point between Europe and Italy. A committed glacier watcher, he made many solo first ascents. Placidus was imprisoned when Switzerland became involved in the wars of the French revolution and used his time to write one of

climbing's first manuals. Instead of introducing climbing as a tool of mountain exploration and science, he came down firmly on the side of climbing for fun. Many Swiss used his advice to put up first ascents in the Bernese Oberland, notably the Jungfrau, as well as the Breithorn and the Monte Rosa.

Chamonix crystal hunters emerged as the first to become professional guides. Even in 1823 the Chamonix company of guides had set themselves up with fixed tariffs for certain climbs in the area. This increased local prosperity had great effect on the local economy, especially in Chamonix, which had few rivals in those days.

In 1850 J.D. Forbes published *Travels Through the Alps* and *A Tour of Mont Blanc and Monte Rosa*, a new breed of books which unashamedly celebrated the joy of climbing. During what has been described as the 'Golden Age of climbing' from 1854 to 1865, most of the big peaks were conquered. But climbing morale

10. Crevasse crossing, Mont Blanc.

was heavily dented by the Whymper tragedy in 1865, when four of the successful summit party were killed on the descent from the Matterhorn.

During the golden age, the vast majority of peak baggers were British. Chief bagger was the Reverend Coolidge, who was a prime topographer of the Alps as claiming to have climbed a staggering 1700 summits. In 1857 the British Alpine Club was formed as a loose association for the society of mountaineers, closely followed by the Austrian Alpine Club in 1862 and the Swiss Alpine Club in 1863, when Thomas Cook brought his first package tour to Switzerland.

The concept of climbing for sport was growing. Most pretensions of scientific research had been abandoned by the English gentry, despite criticisms of being in possession of 'diseased minds'. Some tried to justify the sport as a strengthening of character, a preparation for

battle and adversity. But when it came down to it, the essence of sport as we now understand it is that the enjoyment is justification enough.

The Americans too were early visitors. Howard and Rensselaer climbed Mont Blanc in 1819. Some thought the Alps inferior to their own mountains; others like the Reverend Durkin were so impressed by these manifestations of the power of God that they were cured completely of any mountaineering ambitions whatsoever.

As the Alps were a battleground during the Second World War, recreation stopped dead. But when things opened up again a new wave of climbing skills had been born partly out of military inventiveness, partly out of refusal to be defeated by technical problems. New equipment and clothing forced back the frontiers.

Depending on the ethics involved, it was soon technically possible to bolt, hammer and force a way up just about any route by aided climbing. Often the aids went way beyond any pretension of security on an otherwise unclimbable route. These new routes were not climbable by ordinary techniques, and so the ethics and routes themselves became questionable to many traditionalists.

Also, the concept of new routes on old faces became prevalent. It was not enough for climbers to do only what became known as the 'ordinary route' up a face or a mountain. This was little more than the easiest way to the top. What was now required was the more challenging route – the north face; the north face in winter; the direct route. Climbing became a challenge and a competition. The 'playground of Europe' was only just around the corner.

12. *Climbers camped on the Mer de Glace below the Aiguilles du Midi, Chamonix* (over the page).

CHAPTER FOUR

Alpine People

We hired the only guide left, to lead us on our way. He was over seventy, but he could have given me nine-tenths of his strength and still had all his age entitled him to.
— Mark Twain, *A Tramp Abroad.*

Tourism has been such a steamroller to the people of the Alps that one might be forgiven for thinking that the sole reason for the existence of the 'simple Alpine dweller' is to serve the tourist and reap the undeniable benefits.

Before tourism became a factor, indeed a saviour, life was arduous and existence was 'hand to mouth'. Despite the glories of the Alps and the things which we now see as essentials (for example, guaranteed snow), one can only wonder what kept Alpine dwellers pinned to their meagre existence beyond habit, tradition and nowhere else to go.

Many Swiss travelled far in search of work. They became famous as mercenaries. They sent money home to their families. Before tourism, farming was the only source of income in the Alps. As the mountains came to be explored, crystal and chamois hunters made a precarious living. Then came the Alpine mountain guides, many of whom evolved from chamois hunters when they realized they had valuable skills – local knowledge, mountain and snow craft – to sell to the more adventurous tourist.

Alpine land at altitude was never very profitable and the growing and grazing season was agonizingly short. As rearing cattle and sheep

became less and less profitable, the ties of the working adult with mountain villages became correspondingly weaker. This marginal productivity meant agriculture was largely abandoned in the mid-1800s. As far as industrial life was concerned, the Alpine regions were neither conveniently accessible for the establishment of light industry, nor did they have the manpower to support it. A burgeoning Swiss textile industry in the plains was to bypass the Alps. The problem was worse in Switzerland and Austria, a majority of whose lands were Alpine, than in France or Italy, Germany and Yugoslavia who had viable alternatives. Large parts of the latter countries had nothing to do with the Alps and could aspire to normal economic progress unencumbered by great lumps of rock and vast areas of useless snow.

By the mid-1800s, daily life in the Alps had not changed significantly since the Middle Ages. The Alps, particularly in Switzerland, were almost bankrupt. The best pastures were often occupied with grain harvests, to make the hard Alpine bread which would keep through the winter season. Often a grim Alpine winter was spent mending the tools and preparing for summer, surviving on dried meat, cheese and smoked

13. Beware, state border!

meat. The animals lived inside, on hay. It was in the long winters that the tradition of handicrafts arose in the Alps. There was little else to do when the chores had been done.

Much of the other work in a pre-electric era was the work of preservation. Cheese preserved the milk. Glaciers were even used for chilling milk and preserving meat. Alpine life naturally influenced many of the foods by the methods of preservation, dried meat like Bundner fleisch being a good example in Graubünden.

Although the significance of tourism was not fully grasped in the early stages, it was soon to prove a lifeline for the Alps. This was particularly the case with the development of walking, climbing and skiing as sports for non-Alpine people. Snow, which was once a useless if not dangerous nuisance became better known as 'white gold'.

BORDERS MAY CHANGE – PEOPLE DO NOT

As a mountain range, the Alps have always been indifferent to political borders. Napoleon was nearly ruler of the whole chain and more besides. The empires of Charlemagne and Augustus included the Alps in their time. Borders have changed many times, but languages and customs have not.

Switzerland in the modern era has remained remarkably unaligned, politically and linguistically. Within its borders lingua franca are French, German, Italian and Romansch. But none of these languages will prepare the travellers for the unwritten and arcane colloquial Swiss German. Swiss German dialects can be so varied that communication even between inhabitants of different parts of Switzerland can be difficult. A story goes that two such Schweizers found their only common language was English!

The Western Alps (the French Dauphiné and Savoie) have passed in history through the houses of Burgundy, Savoy, Turin and back to France. Yet French is still spoken in the Italian parts of the watershed.

A large part of what was Austria became Italian after the First World War, changing the nationality of half a million inhabitants. Now famous peaks such as the Drei Zinnen go by the name of the Tre Cime de Lavaredo on the map. But ask a local where the Tre Cime are to be found and he would stare at you in blank incomprehension.

So go the facts of history. But the people change less. One rainy day in Bolzano (Bozen), I met a local farmer tending his vineyards. I am not sure who pressed whom into a glass of the St Magdalena, but the musty dimly lit cellar into which we ducked had been there for 700 years. What can passports and borders say to that? A grape's a grape for all that.

THE LADINS – A FLOURISHING MINORITY

One of the few subdivisions of Alpine people who still retain their traditional lifestyle are the Ladiner people of the South Tirol, now part of Italy. The Ladin people are the smallest racial

14. Shepherd and flock, Dauphiné.

group in the South Tirol, and their dialect belongs to the Rhaeto-Romanic family of languages, nearer to French than Italian. The Rhaeto-Romans are some of the oldest Alpine inhabitants. Today Rhaeto-Romanic is spoken in Switzerland's Graubünden (Romansch), in Italy's Trentino and South Tirol (Ladinish) and in Friaul (Furnlanish). Some 25,000 Ladins live in the Sella group of the Dolomites, in the main valleys of Gröden, Fasser, Gader and Fanes.

Ladinish language is alive and well in the South Tirol – the Ladins use it as their mother tongue. This is helped by their own political organization, which leans more towards Germanic Tirolean culture than Italian. A 1948 law recognized the Ladin right of self-determination, the right to maintain their own traditions, to name their own villages, to speak the language and have their children educated in it at school. In St Martin in Thurn, Ladins have their own cultural institute and newspaper.

But modern pressures are threatening their heritage. Young people look to flatter land to earn a better living. Tourism has invaded the valleys to provide a better living than the harvest ever could. In their brightly coloured traditional costumes, the Ladins themselves have become a tourist attraction. Tradition pays the bills. The summer Ladin festivals are certainly well attended.

TRANSHUMANCE – LIFE OF THE SHEPHERD

The vocational profession of Alpine shepherd is on the wane. Unreliable income and an arduous life hardly encourages recruitment. A typical shepherd, nomadic perhaps by choice, perhaps by necessity, has few possessions, does not own the flock, the pastures, or a house. He lives at the whim of the flock owner. Probably only a few thousand migratory shepherds are still working in the summer months.

Historically, the most profitable use of the summer grazing period is breeding and fattening up for market. Valley markets were visited in

May or early June for the purchase of stock, which were sold again at the end of the season well fattened, it was hoped, on lush Alps. At the end of June a shepherd goes up to the pastures with a couple of dogs and a few hundred sheep belonging to different owners. Awaiting the shepherd and his flock is a steep wind-driven pasture and a tiny wooden cabin.

A few possessions are taken up for the summer – cooking utensils, mementoes, perhaps a cassette recorder and some books and medicines, and that is all for four months of solitude. The average 14-hour day is taken up in constant watching of the herd, keeping them within the limits of the pastures, steering them away from poisonous plants and those with little nutrition, caring for the sick and injured. In October, shortly before the first snows, the shepherd brings the herd down from the high pastures. The shepherd's job is done, as it was in generations before.

This traditional summer migration to the pastures is called transhumance. Animals still travel to the high pastures, but rarely on foot. Most are transported by lorry, but shepherds are still needed in the Alpine pastures.

Many Alpine pastures are communally owned, and are dotted around with small summer huts. On a large alp or series of alps, the lower pastures will be grazed first, the flock travelling higher vertically up the mountain as the summer progresses. There are few villages in the Alps above 2000 m (6500 ft) which are inhabited all the year round. Above this altitude the accommodation is generally seasonal.

One of the most consuming tasks with an Alpine herd, particularly with cows, is milking. Traditionally milk is taken straight from the cow to a cheese-making hut and poured into a huge copper cauldron over a fire. Rennet is added; the curd is put into presses to make cheeses. The cheeses are taken into the valley and stored, often in huts on stilts. As the herd may belong to a number of different owners, the yield is divided proportionally to the ownership.

Mountain cheeses are varied, made with milk from cow, goat or sheep. See the chapter *Food and wine of the Alps* for more detail. You can see cheese being made in Château D'Oex in the Vaudoise Alps of Switzerland.

LIFE OF A MOUNTAIN GUIDE

After the Golden Age of climbing in the mid 1800s, a use had finally been found for the barren summits and crumbling glaciated snowfields of the Alps. Unbelievably to most locals, foreigners actually wanted to visit these places. They had time and money and would pay to be guided to the summits, to have their equipment carried and even at times be carried up themselves in an 'Alpine litter'.

Today the once new but now traditional occupation of guiding is one of the most respected of the Alps. Every town or village with access to climbing has developed a Bureau des Guides or Bergführrerverein, with many guides working throughout the year, either as employees of the guides bureau, the ski school, or self-employed.

Surprisingly this occupation did not, in the early days, come naturally to locals who were as terrified as visitors of the dizzy heights. We hear stories of Saussure, the third man on top of Mont Blanc, having to turn back from a surveying expedition when his 17 guides mutinied, throwing all the food down the mountain. Others forged better reputations – the Taugwalders, Carrel, Guido Rey and Rebuffat have gone down in history as leaders in the profession of leading.

Today's guides are members of an honourable profession which still retains its individuality in an age when this is a rare quality. It is a way of life which still depends on the wind, the snow, the weather, the clouds, and the strength and weakness of the clients. In short the guide works in an elemental world where man cannot dominate the environment and is glad he cannot. Perhaps this is what draws us to the high mountains. And the mountain guide, the

15. Martin Epp, leading Swiss mountain guide.

teacher, the leader, the Alpinist, is the prime working exponent of enjoying the mountains for what they are.

One of the most famous companies of guides – the Chamonix company of guides – was set up in 1823, and is still something of a closed shop. Non-Chamoniards are only accepted after stringent selection procedures. Tradition is strong, as on the 15th of August annually when all the guides must be present for a climbing demonstration and the blessing of their ice-axes. Other well known guide companies in France are those of L'Oisans, Pralognan and Grenoble in the pre-Alps. In Switzerland the Grindelwald, Zermatt and Andermatt guides are famous; in Italy, those of Courmayeur and Val Gardena, in Austria the guides of Heiligenblut.

If a guide has work, he is generally away from home for long periods, requiring great patience and forbearance from his wife and family. If he has little work, he may be hanging around the house complaining about the weather and the lack of clients. He is just as likely to ring up a friend, jump in a battered old car and travel to a part of the Alps where the weather is better and

climb a favourite peak purely for the fun of it.

Either way it is a difficult existence. Most Alpine guides are also trained as ski instructors, so that during the winter months they have more or less guaranteed income in the employ of the local ski school. But not every ski instructor is qualified as a mountain guide. Many ski instructors have other jobs in the summer, such as farming or running a tourist hotel.

Even today the traditional Alpine professions are compromised by the basic need to earn a living. It may be an idyll to have one's fortunes blow with the wind, but the facts of modern life are that even the resilient inhabitants of Alpine villages demand a minimum standard of living.

In God's country, the inhabitants of the Alps have thanked God for tourism and skiing. But how can traditional forms of occupation survive in the face of the rich pickings of tourism?

The ski lift trade and industries, the hotel and travel trade have brought a huge influx to Alpine villages when a hundred years ago they were deserted and almost bankrupt. An Alpine village with a population of 5000 may easily accommodate two or three times that amount in busy periods. They cannot all live in quaint Alpine wooden chalets.

The ski trade has been particularly bad in throwing up vast satanic tower blocks which scar the landscape but nourish and shelter the villagers. However, they are as likely to fill the pocket of a developer in Paris or Lyon. These are in stark contrast to the traditional chalets. The modern approach varies. Many attractive new buildings echo old styles and show pride in their heritage, others flaunt all standards of aesthetics and Alpine heritage.

POPULAR ALPINE FESTIVALS AND CUSTOMS

Swiss Folk festivals

Hallwill is one of the best places to witness the Swiss winter customs, which begin with the

Chlauswettchloepfe, a whip-cracking contest at the end of November. Six of the best whip-cracking boys then have the honour of chasing St Nicholas. At Christmas the girls accompany a Christmas child on a carol-singing tour of the village. On New Year's eve symbolic threshing sees the New Year in. Whipcrackers also accompany the pursuit of St Nicholas on December 5 at Kussnacht am Rigi.

Pre-Lenten carnival is widely celebrated in Switzerland (as in other Alpine countries), in February and the days leading up to Ash Wednesday. The grotesque carnival masks of the Lötschental carnival parade are professionally carved and much sought after as souvenirs. Lucerne also celebrates carnival, as does the Italian/Swiss district of Ticino in the south at Bellinzona. Probably the largest carnival celebration in Switzerland is the non-Alpine carnival in Basel, with some 15,000 masked participants.

The *Landsgemeinden*, the annual assemblies of qualified voters, usually take place on the last Sunday of April or the first Sunday of May. These occur in some of the cantons of central and eastern Switzerland, Schwyz and canton Graubünden, where a form of direct democracy only possible in the smaller areas exists. A few thousand voters congregate in the open to select representatives for cantonal offices and debate matters of cantonal importance. Voting is done by a show of hands and an exact count where there is no clear majority.

The most famous of these is the Landesgemeinde in Appenzell where the men are obliged to carry a sword, and the women have no vote on cantonal affairs, although they do vote on federal affairs. In Stans, the signal to walk to the meeting place outside the town is given by blowing a horn, a reminder of an ancient call to battle. In Glarus, the children are allowed to stand within the ring of the voters, to learn their future duties.

In the Valais as well as in the Aosta valley of Italy, June is the time to see spontaneous cow fights. August 1 is celebrated in the cantons as Swiss National Day. This commemorates the first agreement between Uri, Schwyz and Unterwalden cantons which formed the basis of the present Confederation Helvetica.

The harvest festivals were, of course, of particular significance to Alpine dwellers. If the harvest was good, the village would survive another winter. At the end of September or beginning of October, Neuchâtel (stretching the Alps a little) and Lugano have vintage festivals. The latter co-ordinates much of the wine-growing activities of French-speaking Switzerland as well as the older Lugano flower festival. Canton Unterwalden at the end of October or beginning of November celebrates the end of the Alpine summer and gives thanks for a good harvest.

Swiss Alpine museums

The Swiss Open Air Museum. CH–3855 Brienz (tel 036/511442). Situated in Ballenberg near Brienz in the Bernese Oberland. The main types of houses and settlements in Switzerland are shown in life-size scale. There is also a shop for traditional crafts.

Traditional costumes. Embroidery and accordions can be seen at the **Trachten Museum**, Utenberg CH–6000 Luzern (tel 041/36 80 58).

The way of life of the people of Appenzell. **Appenzell Museum**, Museum for Appenzeller Brauchtum, Dorfplatz CH–9107 Urnasch (tel 071/58 23 22).

Natural history and culture of the Swiss Alps, mountaineering and maps, **Swiss Alpine Museum**, Helvetiaplatz 4 CH–3005 Bern (tel 031/43 04 34).

The Glacier Garden: 20 million years of the earth's history, Gletschergarten, Denkmalstrasse 4, CH–6006 Luzern (tel 041/51 43 40).

16. *Ladin people's folk festival, Dolomites.*

Viticulture. History of wine growing. **Musée Vaudois de la vigne et du vin**, Château, CH–1860 Aigle (tel 025/26 21 30).

Musée de la Vigne et du vin, Château, CH–2017 Boudry (tel 038/42 10 98).

National Dairy Museum. How Switzerland became the land of cheese, how the cheese got its holes, **Nationales Milchwirtschaftliches Museum**, CH–3117 Kiesen (tel 031/45 33 31).

Alpine rooms, paper silhouettes, local history, **Musée du Vieux Pays d'Enhaut**, Les Bossons CH–1837 Château d'Oex (tel 029/46520).

The Engadine Museum, St Moritz, original wooden panelled rooms collected under one roof.

Collection of steam locomotives and electrically driven trains, **Musée vivant de fer Blonay**, Chamby CH–1807 Blonay (tel 021/38 29 40).

Sherlock Holmes Museum, including a re-construction of the living room of Sherlock Holmes. He has a great Swiss following ever since Conan Doyle used the falls of Reichenbach as the final scene in *Memoirs* for the showdown between Holmes and Moriarty. **Musée Sherlock Holmes**, Château, CH–1522 Lucens (tel 021/95 80 32)

Swiss clocks. 3000 or so at the **Musée International d'horlogerie**, 29 Rue des Musées, CH–2300 La Chaux de Fonds (tel 039 23 62 63).

Collection of timepieces, from 1400 BC to the present day, **Museum der Zeitmessung Beyer**, Bahnhofstrasse 31, CH–8001 Zürich (tel 01/221 10 80).

French Alpine festivals

Early December – Criterium International Première Neige at Val D'Isère, the start of the ski World Cup season.
December – Festival of true adventure films.
January – Festival of 'films of the fantastic'.
Mid July – Chambéry, world folklore festival.
August – Mountain Guides festival in Chamonix.
– Fête du Lac Annecy.
– Flower festival in Aix les Bains.
July, August – Pralognan, Alpine guide festival.
September – Ugine, Fête ds Montagnes.
October – Chambéry, Alpine salon.

French Alpine museums

Musee Savoisien Chambéry. Archaeology, ethnography, art and history of Savoie (tel 79 33 44 48).

Natural History Museum, Chambéry (tel 79 33 22 09).

Maison Rouge, Conflans. Archaeology, Savoyard furniture, traditional life (tel 79 32 57 42).

Mont Cenis, Centre de documentation alpin. Quality works on the national parks of the Vanoise, Haute Maurienne, the mountain environment, topographical guides, books and cassettes, CIS, Maison de La Montagne 73480 Lanslebourg, Mont Cenis, Chambéry (tel 79 05 92 30).

Centre D'Animation Vanoise. Life in the Vanoise, Alpine fauna, mountain life, Quartier Napoleon, 73480 Lanslebourg, Mont Cenis (tel 79 05 91 57).

Cooperative Laitiers du Beaufortin. Reconstruction of an Alpine chalet, slide show on how Beaufortin cheese, the 'prince of gruyères', is made, and why the French cannot produce cheese with holes. 73270 Beaufort (tel 79 31 20 30).

Maison de la Montagne, Musée Alpin Chamonix. History of the Chamonix valley and the conquest of the Alpine summits. Documents and historic photographs, historic climbing apparatus too, including a parasol carried by none other than the great Saussure. Alpine crystals and paintings. La Residence Av Croz, 74400 Chamonix (tel 50 53 25 95).

Montenvers Crystal Gallery, Alpine zoo in summer, marmots, chamois and numerous mountain animals. **Musée Montagnard.** Place de L'Église 74310 Les Houches (tel 50 55 50 62).

Italian Alpine festivals and museums

The Ladiner festivals, summer and autumn, South Tirol.

St Ulrich, Casa di Ladins. House of the Ladins, past and present folklore Bozen, Sparkassenstrasse, town museum, Tirolean dresses and domestic objects.

Ringberg castle and wine museum (tel 0471 31723).

Burgstall animal species museum.

Meran town museum. Minerals, prehistoric objects and traditional dresses from Meran.

German Alpine folk events and museums

Garmisch Partenkirchen. Peasants' Theatre.

Adelsheim Castle, Berchtesgaden, built in 1614, is today the home of a folk museum containing a unique collection of the art and culture of the Berchtesgadener Land.

Berchtesgadener Folk Theatre, Franziskanerplatz. Daily performances, Thursdays, Fridays and Saturdays in winter. For the theatre programme – tel 08652/2858.

Austrian Alpine festivals

Fasnacht festivals precede the rigours of Lent, with gypsy costumes and masks.

At Easter in the Kaisergebirge, there are intermittent passion plays at Erl and Thiersee.

On the Sunday after Easter, Virger Widderprozession in Virgental East Tirol, Virgen, to the pilgrimage church at Obermauer.

17. Berchtesgaden folk music.

July and August annually – Salzburg Mozart festival.

Summer – widespread celebrations on Corpus Christi days (Fronleichnam) and Assumption (Maria Himmelfahrt) in August.

End of August or early September – the spectacular *Almabtrieb*: herders bring their cattle down from the mountain pastures for winter, led by the most productive cow festooned with ribbons.

Austrian Alpine museums

Tiermuseum 'Heimisches Wild', Burgstall, 360 types of stuffed Tirolean wildlife (tel 0473/291126).

Dorf Tirol Brunnenburg Landwirtschaftliches Museum. Films and documents on agriculture, art, folklore (tel 0473/93533).

Sudtiroler Weinmuseum. Wine museum. Kaltern an der Weinstrasse (tel 0471/963169).

Schloss Tirol. Excellent exhibition on Tirolean history (tel 0473/34021).

Tiroler Volkskunstmuseum, Innsbruck. Museum of popular arts, insights into the everyday life of old Tirol, housed in an old Franciscan monastery, one of the best examples of a Heimatmuseum.

Fulpmes, Stubaital, famous for manufacture of mountain climbing equipment, **Blacksmith's Museum** Schmiedermuseum.

Hall im Tirol, Bergbaumuseum. Saltmining museum, for salt for food preservation.

Schwaz Heimatsmuseum. Folk museum.

Kitzbühel Heimatmuseum. Folk museum.

Kufstein Heimatmuseum. Relics of giant bears from 30,000 BC, hunted by earliest inhabitants of the area.

Alpine Association Museum. Wilhelm Greil Strasse 15, Innsbruck.

Alpbach. Mountain farming museum.

St Anton am Arlberg. Ski and folk museum; history of skiing in the Arlberg region.

Wildschönau. Alpine farming museum in the Oberau fire brigade building.

Yugoslav Alpine festivals and museums

Ilidza (near Sarajevo), summer folk music festival.

Triglav National Park museum.

Slovene geological trail. In the mountains, geological pathways are marked with yellow arrows and crossed hammers pointing out points of geological interest.

CHAPTER FIVE

The Natural Life of the Alps

*They took all the trees and put them in a tree museum, And charged the
people a dollar and a half just to see them*
— Joni Mitchell.

*That evening, when the sun dipped behind the earth, I experienced a deep
feeling of serenity in the presence of so many natural things; the wood fire, the
valley which drew us on, the magnetic mountains, the air of peace and silence,
the living sky. I was happy to be there; and thinking of my boyhood, of my
very first excursion in the mountains, so like the one we were making now. I
said to myself again; 'It's just like the first time'*
— Gaston Rebuffat.

It is easy to think of the Alps as having unlimited
space to be enjoyed by animals and humans
alike. This may have been the case 200 years ago,
but not today. Formerly isolated mountain
villages soon shook from the heavy footfall of
the tourist. Railways and cable cars thrust into
the upper valleys. Roads conquered the great
passes and the highest peaks of the Alps – too
mighty even for Alpine roadbuilders – were
disembowelled by tunnels. Pistes were laid out
and lift pylons scarred the skies. Mountain
villagers now live most of the year far outnum-
bered by the hoardes of visitors. Their social
structure has been destroyed but the perils of
Alpine farming have been replaced by a relatively secure income from tourism.

Put bluntly, where profit dictates the mountains have been opened up, and nature has come
close to the brink of ruin. But the forces of
conservation have begun to win the odd skirmish
in the continuing war against progress. A
national park here, a plant preservation zone
there – these are hailed as major advances, and
they are. But public awareness of the fragility of

nature at high altitude still needs to be increased.

The balance of nature is delicate everywhere
in the world, and nowhere more so than around
the snowline in the Alps. Only species which
have evolved specific skills have survived the
severe selection process of evolution. The chamois, one of the best known Alpine animals, has
been decimated by man, and survives now only
under rigorous protection, as does the best
known Alpine flower, the edelweiss. The last
Alpine wolf was killed over 50 years ago. Bears
survive only by rumour, although some can be
seen living in a concrete pit in the centre of Berne.
Man is the single greatest threat to the natural
life of the Alps.

ALPINE ANIMALS

The animals you are most likely to see in the Alps
are cows, sheep and goats, rather than anything
wild. Wherever you are, your ears will ring with
cowbells. But here are a few animals and birds
which may be seen in the Alps. (Also seen in the
Alps are animals such as fox, badger, squirrel,

and many birds, which although they are seen in the Alps, are not truly Alpine.)

The Chamois has a remarkable instinct for self-preservation above the snow-line, seeming to be able to spot and avoid slopes with avalanche danger. It shares some of the characteristics of the antelope and the goat. Its black horns are about 6 in (15 cm) long and curve sharply backwards. In summer the coat is reddish brown, but as winter approaches it becomes almost black. Their summer range is up to about 3500 m (11,500 ft), when they live in

18. The lake, Bled, Yugoslavia.

herds of 10–20, grazing under the watchful eye of a lookout. The mating season begins at the end of October and young are born about May. Chamois, we discover, are really bed bugs, says Mark Twain.

The Ibex was hunted almost to extinction at the end of the eighteenth century for its beauty and its supposed powers of healing. Their Alpine presence was re-established in parts of the Alps from a small surviving herd in the Gran Paradiso in Italy. They stand some 3 ft (1 m) high, 5 ft (1.6 m) long and weigh up to 200 lbs (90 kg) and have long curved horns up to 3 ft (1 m) long. Very sure-footed, they are outstanding athletes on sheer rock, ascending in a couple of bounds what might take a good human climber a few minutes of technical climbing. They mate in early December and the young are born in May or June. Grass and lichen are their main foods.

The **Moufflon** was introduced into the Alps from its native Sardinia and Corsica, and has become well established in places, living in herds of 20 or so animals. Rams in good condition have impressive rounded horns, which are put to good use in fierce rutting fights in October, November and December. Young are born in April or May.

The **Pine Marten** is found in most Alpine regions, but still is fairly rare. It favours coniferous woods, nesting in the trees. This fur-covered predator, which measures about three foot from head to tail, hunts mostly at night. After nine months' gestation, young are born blind. The marten often marks its territory with a strong smell.

The **Marmot**. Relative of the squirrel and dormouse, the marmot likes open slopes between 1400 m (4500 ft) and 2600 m (8500 ft), where it can burrow and keep a good lookout. About 2 ft (60 cm) long, the marmot is thick-set and rabbit coloured, with long whiskers and broad sharp teeth. They live in large colonies in extensive burrows 6 ft (2 m) below ground. When hibernating in winter, their body temperature drops from 37°C (100°F) to 5°C (41°F). On waking in spring they mate and produce babies in a month. Their eyesight is good and they whistle and run for cover if danger comes too near.

The **Alpine Hare** resembles a plains hare but is a little smaller. In winter the coat turns white except for the tips of the ears. It lives at an altitude of about 2000 m (6500 ft). It partially hibernates in winter, allowing itself to be covered by snow, emerging when the snow is hard enough for it to support itself on spreading paws. It bears some five leverets twice a year.

The **Ptarmigan** is rarely seen at close quarters. It can be found above 2200 m (7000 ft) and is similar in size to a pheasant. In summer it is mostly brown, in autumn grey, and becomes pure white in winter. Spring mating plumage is white, black and red. In cold weather the bird crouches down and lets itself be buried in the snow until conditions have improved.

The **Blackcock** can be found at altitudes up to 2600 m (8500 ft) well up to the tree line. Its summer colour is very dark brown. It measures about three feet long. The blackcock and grey hen mate in April to June, after an elaborate dawn courtship display. They return to the same mating ground every year and in winter hole up in the snow during bad weather.

The **Alpine Chough** is very dark blue with a yellow beak and red legs, about a foot long. It is a sociable bird which lives in large colonies up to 4200 m (13,500 ft). It nests in holes in the rock, rears its young in July and eats anything.

The **Griffon Vulture** is a regular summer visitor to the Alps, particularly to Salzburg and Carinthia. It stays from May till September although it does not breed in the Alps, but in its native Balkans. It likes warm southern slopes, suns itself for hours, and has keen eyesight which enables it to spot prey from a great height. It can be up to 3 ft (1 m) long with a wingspan of 10 ft (3 m), and is quite rare.

The **Golden Eagle** nests in inaccessible spots below the tree line, hunting in pairs and remaining in the same area for life. The male is smaller than the female, with a length of 3 ft (1 m), wingspan 6 ft (2 m).

Other birds of prey seen in the Alps are the buzzard, the peregrine falcon, kestrel and sparrow hawk.

ANIMAL MANNERS FOR OFF-PISTE SKIERS

Off-piste and powder skiers can – quite unwittingly – be a weapon of destruction for tomorrow's forests and today's mountain animals. The more people are converted to the joys of skiing nature's wild side, the more potential damage can be done to the flora and fauna. Yet this situation can so easily be avoided with a little knowledge of the facts of animal life above the snowline in winter.

Summer or winter, animals spend the majority of their lives foraging for food. Because of the shrinkage of their habitat, it is even more important that wildlife is able to forage without disturbance. In winter the need for nutrition is greater, the daylight hours are shorter and the available food is less. The ski season, welcomed by humans, is a stressful time for animals.

Wild animals are very sparing with their energy in winter. Evolution and natural selection has ensured that the free-living animals indigenous to the Alps are well adjusted to the rigours of the winter. But dealing with the human factor is something to which they may never learn to adjust.

Their husbandry of energy shows a definite yearly cycle. In the summer when vegetation grows freely they are on the move and feed vigorously. Energy is stored in the form of fat. In winter what little vegetation exists is hard to reach because of the snow cover. They have to live mainly off their reserves. In particular, pregnant animals bear an even greater burden in having to nourish the embryo which, if they survive, will be born in spring or summer.

It is tempting to think that disturbing wild animals in winter amounts to little more than trivial antisociality. But their chances of survival, even without disturbance, are so delicate that even a few alarmed flights in a winter can mean death. Fleeing animals use up vast energy reserves when frightened in winter, particularly if they have to run through deep snow, where, if we are skiing off piste, we are most likely to disturb them.

Animals are less bothered by ascending parties, which are slow and noisy and give plenty of warning. The real danger lies when a party of downhill skiers explodes into their habitat at 30 mph (60 kph). Seconds before, all was peace and tranquillity. They run for their lives through the deep snow, burning up in a moment fat reserves which their bodies had set aside to get them through the next week. Those fat reserves cannot be replaced until spring.

Neither must the trees be forgotten. Woodland at high altitude hinders erosion, diverts high-level flooding and reduces avalanche risk. Old trees which are damaged cannot be saved. But the saplings of today will be the forests of tomorrow. It may be a good ten or twenty years before a tree is large enough to gain the respect of the skier (i.e. it is big enough to hurt), but when they are young they are in most need of careful treatment. Powder skiers are the greatest danger for young trees, which make handy natural slalom gates to make a turn around. Yet sharp ski edges can easily sever twigs, bark and branches, killing the tree.

As ski resorts grow, animal habitat shrinks. Some resorts display notices about new plantations and forestry areas where animals like to spend the winter. For example, Klosters and Sorenberg in Switzerland have pilot schemes designating a number of 'green areas' which fall into this category. There is absolutely no restriction on entering these forests. The off-piste skier is merely asked to respect the inhabitants and disturb them as little as possible.

In Germany, the DAV ('Deutsche Alpen Verein') issues a useful leaflet for ski tourers and powder skiers, giving pointers for off-piste manners in such areas. These include:

1. Take note of markings for footpaths and pistes.
2. Do not make unnecessary climbing tracks if there already exists a reasonable uphill path.
3. Avoid virgin slopes if wild animals could be disturbed. If you see tracks then you must assume the presence of animals. Slopes free from trees and projecting rocks are preferable since they are free from animal habitats.

North and north-western slopes, on which chamois tend not to go, are also preferable.

4. If you spot wild animals from a distance, give them a wide berth. If this is not possible, make your presence known without alarming them. Maintaining a conversation at normal volume should be enough. Avoid surprising or stalking them, so that they do not panic and bolt.

5. If you suddenly come upon a wild animal, back away and keep your distance.

6. Avoid places where animals are fed in winter by villagers.

7. Animal watching in winter is best done in late afternoon through a long telescope or binoculars.

8. Wherever possible avoid woods. If you have to go through them, use paths or roads. Very young plantations should be avoided. When turning in woods be particularly careful not to cut trees with the edges of your skis.

In this over-regulated world, no-one would seek to make these anything but voluntary guidelines for off-piste skiers. But if skiers do think about them from time to time, at least they can enjoy the powder with a clearer conscience.

ALPINE PLANTS

Above the height of the average Alpine resort, say 1500 m (5000 ft), the Alpine treeline is close to 2000 m (6500 ft). To the north of the main chain it may be 300 m (1000 ft) lower, to the south 300 m higher. The highest altitude trees in the Alps tend to be pines and spruces, but above the treeline is the true domain of the Alpine plant. Conifers reach their upper limit of about 2600 m (8500 ft), shrubs persist up to the summer snowline at about 3200 m (10,500 ft). Hay meadows can be found up to about 2000 m (6500 ft), while Alpine pastures can go as high as 3000 m (10,000 ft). Limestone seems to support a higher number of species than harder rocks such as granite.

Above the treeline the battle for survival is

19. *Autumn, Dauphiné.*

hard-fought indeed. Plants tend to become smaller and more compact than their lower altitude relations and are all creeper plants. Thus they use what heat is available, minimize the exposure to cold, extremes of temperature and dehydration. Roots tend to be strong for maximum water collection and security. Flowering and seeding need to happen very quickly indeed in the short summer season. Only five per cent or so are high altitude annuals or biennials since a bad summer could easily interfere with re-seeding.

The very highest limit of plant life is about 4700 m (15,000 ft), where the occasional lichen can still grow under the snow. Despite the obviously arduous conditions, Alpine flowers do survive and provide a wonderful covering, some 700 species, in the summer months. Some even have the strength to push up through the snow, like Alpine snowbells. Other spectacular and colourful performers are the Alpenrose, the Monkshood and the Gentian. You may see wild plants and animals in most unspoiled areas in the Alps, but there are many places where Alpine zoos have been established and semi-wild Alpine gardens encouraged to flourish.

20. *Richardière and Mont Aiguille, Dauphiné Alps
– the typical lightly wooded landscape of the
lower Alps in autumn.*

THE POLITICS OF POLLUTION

Some eight million people reside permanently in the Alps. Another ten million have holiday homes. Forty million visitors spend a total of 250 million tourist days in the Alps every year, making the Alps, according to the International Union for the Conservation of Nature and Natural Resources, the most threatened mountain range in the world. Physical pollution and air pollution pose an equal threat. Temperature inversions hold fetid industrial air down in the valleys. The rubbish produced by 40 million visitors has to go somewhere, and locals are not always long-sighted in disposing of it. At peak periods in summer, 50,000 vehicles cross the Brenner pass between Austria and Italy.

Forests ail and lose their grip, landslides and avalanches become more common because of lack of essential forestry protection. This is not an angry fiction; the fact is that in the summer of 1988 in the Alps, 60 people lost their lives, and hundreds lost their homes in landslides which would have been avoided had the forests been in good condition. Countries pride themselves on their kilometerage of railways and ski runs, while nature's statistics are on the run. Almost every skiable mountain is capped by ski lifts, whose scarring effect is all the worse in summer.

Even that most ecological of sports, walking, causes problems. Pathways above 2000 m (6500 ft) are easily eroded and slow to heal, so hard is it for vegetation to grow again when damaged.

Yet visitors come, and the development continues. National Parks have been set up: areas of protection designated for flora and fauna. The conservation movement is laudable, but is it only the national parks (a tiny fraction of the Alps) which are to remain protected?

What can we do?: insist on unleaded petrol, take home litter, stay on the path, contribute to ecological causes, not pick flowers and frighten animals, only camp where allowed, not bring dogs into national parks, and take care with cigarettes and camp fires.

GARDENS

Alpine Botanical Garden Section Museum, Viote di Monte Bondone, Trento, Italy.
Austrian Alpine flower garden, Kitzbüheler Horn, Austria.
Dauphiné Alpine plant reserve, France.
Jardin Alpin Jaysinia, Samoëns, France.
Aiguilles Rouges Nature reserve, France.
Juliana Alpinetum, Triglav, Yugoslavia.

For detailed reading on Alpine flowers, see *Mountain Flowers of Europe*, Huxley 1967/86, Blandford.

ALPINE ZOOS

Merlet Animal Park, Route de Merlet et des Houches, Chamonix.
Alpine zoo, Montenvers, Mer de Glace.
Natural history museum, Chambéry (79 33 22 09).
Centre D'Animation Vanoise, life in the Vanoise, Alpine fauna, mountain life, Quartier Napoleon, 73480 Lanslebourg, Mont Cenis (tel 79 05 91 57).
Tiermuseum 'Heimisches Wild', Burgstall, 360 types of stuffed Tirolean wildlife (tel 0473/291126).
Ferleiten wildlife park, Glocknerstrasse, Fusch, Austria.
Innsbruck Alpine Zoo, Austria.
Aurach Wildlife Park, Kitzbühel Alps.

MAIN PROTECTED ALPINE AREAS

France: Parc National de la Vanoise; Parc national des Écrins; Parcs naturels regionaux, Vercors and Queyras; Reserve Naturelle des Aiguilles Rouges.
Switzerland: Swiss National Park, Engadin.
Italy: Gran Paradiso National Park; Brenta Natural Park; Ortler.
Germany: Berchtesgaden National Park.
Austria: Hohe Tauern National Park.
Yugoslavia: Triglav National Park.

CHAPTER SIX

Visiting the Alps

But our vivid and day-long consciousness of the mountain, of each other, and of the drama which we and the mountain played out at length together, cannot be faithfully reproduced. It even escaped all but our general recollection. The mountaineer returns to his hills because he remembers always that he has forgotten so much.
— Geoffrey Winthrop Young.

From the USA travellers will usually only have the option of arriving by air on flights routed via London or Paris, or direct to a major airport in one of the Alpine countries. Flying is also the quickest way from the UK, but the question is, having arrived, how will you get around?

In most Alpine countries, particularly Switzerland and Austria, local connections are excellent by bus, train or even boat. If you have a specific destination in mind, this may be the right choice. Local transport can also be a lot of fun even if you wish to travel around to different locations, or walk from one valley to the next, but you will need to allow plenty of time for this.

Once the traveller leaves the plains and gets into the mountains proper, traditional concepts of travel times lose all relevance. Even on good roads and established railway lines, tiny map distances can take all day. The basic rule is not to try to cram too much into your Alpine holiday or a disproportionate amount of time will be spent travelling.

Renting a car at the airport is certainly convenient, efficient and can be arranged from home. On a long trip the expense can be considerable. Travelling from the UK or Europe by car may be the cost-effective answer if you are planning a longish stay and want the convenience of your own transport or can share the expenses. One pressing reason for having a car is that, summer or winter, the great variety of Alpine sporting and outdoor possibilities mean you could want to bring your skis, climbing gear, tennis kit, windsurfer, hang-glider and expect to use them all in the same ten-day period. Try fitting that into a 20 kg baggage allowance! From the UK a ferry or hovercraft crossing lasting half an hour to one and a half hours will have to be added to a typical journey time of Calais–Chamonix (10–12 hours), Calais–Zermatt (12–14 hours).

One of the cheapest ways to reach the Alps from the UK is by train. In Europe, the Inter-rail card is valid for the under 26s for one month's unlimited travel. For visitors originating outside Europe, the Eurailpass offers discounted first class travel with further discounts for the under 26s in the form of the Eurail Youth Pass. In the USA both must be purchased before departure. The disadvantage with these passes is that they

do not cover all Alpine railways and cable cars. Many countries have their own internal rail passes, very good value and convenient. The TGV from Paris arrives in Lyon in 3½ hours, but it is not cheap. See *The Alps by Train* for more details.

Buses are also a cheap way to arrive in the Alps, especially from the UK. The disadvantage is that you often arrive tired and need a day to recover, although many have sleeping facilities on board. Local buses in the Alps are also fun and cheap. Many English and American companies run organized bus tours through the Alps, which can be convivial and comprehensive and absolve the traveller from the need to do any planning whatsoever.

Some countries, e.g. Switzerland, have combined holiday passes either for specific areas or the whole country. For example, the Swiss

21. *The ideal personalised numberplate from the Alps!*

holiday card gives unlimited travel on any combination of bus, train or boat.

Alpine time

Most Alpine countries use the 24-hour clock: Los Angeles 6am (0600), New York 9am (0900), London 2pm (1400), the Alps 3pm, (1500).

Insurance

Comprehensive travel insurance is recommended, to include loss of baggage, personal effects and delay/cancellation. Be sure to have full winter sports coverage and mountaineering extensions where appropriate, since a mountain rescue bill can run into thousands of pounds or dollars.

Money

Eurocheques, available from your bank, are extremely useful in the Alps, both for cashing money and for making purchases. The advantage is that they can be written in any foreign currency for the equivalent of £100 per day.

Weather and the Alpine seasons

The Alps are one of the great climatic barriers of the world. The north has a wetter and colder climate, since Atlantic polar maritime or returning polar maritime air masses are forced to rise and dump rain or snow on the northern side. The south of the Alpine chain is clearer and drier, with a more Mediterranean climate. Many times when bad weather has been set firm for some time in the Bernese Oberland, a short trip south through the Gotthard tunnel to Ticino will find spring weather in Lugano or Locarno, with temperatures 5°C–10°C warmer on the southern side for the same elevation.

In general the east near Vienna and the south have the driest summer weather. In winter snowfall is heaviest to the west and north of the Alps and lies longer on the ground because of the lower temperatures. The winter snowline in a true Alpine resort is well down to 1000 m (3300 ft) or below, whereas in summer it may be 2500 m (8000 ft) or well above. Bear these figures in mind when planning any journey by car in the Alps. Snow deep enough to close the highest passes can linger well into June and threaten them any time after October. Early and late season walkers may also be taken by surprise by the snowline and should have with them the relevant equipment (see the walking chapter.) At any time of year it is possible to have snow above 2000 m (6500 ft) and above 3500 m (11,500 ft) rain is almost never seen at any time of year.

When to visit

Mountain weather is even less predictable than that of the plains. Whereas ten years ago it might have been safe to plan a ski holiday any time after the beginning of December, more recently Christmas skiers have needed to pack their walking boots. The current trend is for the real winter snow to arrive later each year so that winter lingers on well into May at altitude.

People tend to visit the Alps either to ski in winter or to take advantage of many of the summer activities. Late spring and autumn are often neglected by the visitor and are regarded as holiday time or 'dead season' by the locals. Conversely they are the quietest times to visit the Alps.

The Alpine year

Very roughly the year can be divided as follows:

December through to early April is the official skiing season for piste skiing, depending on snow conditions. Christmas, New Year and Easter are always very busy in resorts with locals and tourists alike, queues are long, roads and airports busy. Booking ahead for accommodation is essential. The weather is often sunny high in the ski resorts throughout winter, and a tan is possible at any time. In valleys, mountains may make the day much shorter. Some north faces hardly see the sun in winter.

January is a quieter month when good skiing can be had. The middle of February becomes busy again with local school holidays clogging the pistes. Make enquiries with tourist offices as to the dates which are often staggered in different parts of the country and can effectively mar an otherwise good skiing month. March becomes quieter again until the Easter crowds build up. After Easter, depending on whether it is early or late, good skiing can be had well into April until the resorts close.

March, April, May and even June are good months for skiiing off piste, ski mountaineering and ski touring on glaciers at high altitude. See the skiing chapter.

Depending on altitude and the weather, spring starts any time from late February to late April in the valleys. Alpine flowers follow the snowline up the mountains. Spring (April, May and June) can be a wonderful time to visit, with lengthening days and fairly stable weather. But glaciers and high walking routes will still be well covered with snow.

Weather in the summer months of July and August is frequently unsettled. Cloud shrouds the summits and obliterates high mountain views, while the valleys are sunny. Summer skiing is still possible on many glaciers in June and July, while at valley level the variety of outdoor sports is prodigious.

There is a tendency for weather around September to be clearer and more stable, even into October. But the Alps can be just as busy for tourism in August and September, so again beware of school and national holidays when making your plans. September is a favourite time for walking because of the stable weather and the fact that the snowline has receded on glaciers and summer walking and climbing routes.

November is the 'dead' season, when téléfériques only run intermittently, hoteliers board up their windows, re-decorate the rooms, take their own holidays, or just sit in bars and talk about the tourist harvest. The weather depends on whether winter comes early or late. It can be clear, dry and snowless, with most car passes open. Or winter may arrive overnight and close the passes until the spring. On balance this is a time when skies are overcast and brooding, hoteliers are amazed to see you and finding an open hotel in an Alpine resort can be difficult. Basically in November the Alps are closed.

Alpine winds

Certain Alpine valleys, particularly those running from south to north experience a very warm dry wind called the *föhn*, which may blow from 20 to 40 days a year. It is most frequent in spring and autumn when it can melt snow with prodigious speed and bring sudden avalanche risk. The air can become so dry during the *föhn* that there is serious fire risk in the forests and to wooden buildings. This warm air comes from the south of the Alps and is warmed and dried as the Alpine barrier forces it to rise and then descend on the northern side. Warm winds can also originate as far away as the Sahara. It is by no means uncommon to see a thin film of yellow sand coating the glaciers and high snowfields. Glaciologists can identify the date of these winds centuries ago from layers in the ice.

Prevailing winter winds are often from the south and south-west, dumping snow on north and east slopes. The coldest Alpine conditions in winter usually occur with east to north-east winds bringing in very low temperatures from Eastern Europe and Russia.

THE FRENCH ALPS AT A GLANCE

Main Alpine ranges: Maritime, Cottian, Dauphiné, Graian.

Highest and best known summits: Mont Blanc (4807 m/15,771 ft – highest in Europe), La Meije (3983 m/13,067 ft), Mont Aiguille (2086 m/6844 ft) – one of the first recorded climbs, in 1492.

Best known Alpine towns/resorts. Chamonix for Mont Blanc and the Aiguilles du Midi cable car (3842 m/12,605 ft), the British and the skiing; Val D'Isère/Tignes for skiing.

Other physical features: The Vallée Blanche and the Mer de Glace, world-famous scenic glaciated off-piste ski run at Chamonix.

Main Lakes: Geneva, Annecy, Le Bourget, Aiguebellette.

Tourist Offices
London, 178 Piccadilly, London W1V 0AL, tel (071) 491 7622.
New York, 610 Fifth Avenue, New York, NY 10017.

Embassies/Consulates
British, 16 Rue D'Anjou, 75008 Paris, tel (1) 42 66 91 42, and Toulouse.

Visas
British passport holders – no visa.
USA passport holders – visa required.

Languages
French, some English spoken in larger resorts.

Currency
French Franc, 100 centimes. £1.00 is around 10 francs, $1 is about 6.50 FF. Credit cards and Eurocheques widely accepted. Banks 9–1200, 1400–1600 weekdays. Some have Monday closing too.

Electricity
220 volt AC; take a European plug adapter.

Accommodation
Traditional French hotels are generally cheap. Newer Alpine tower blocks and apartments tend to be cramped and less attractive. Food is mostly excellent. Self-catering is the cheapest for a large group or families. Gîtes, accommodation in local farmhouses, can be charming.

Air travel
Geneva airport is shared with Switzerland and forms a convenient access to the Mont Blanc and Savoie area. Grenoble and Lyon (Satolas) are also convenient for the Dauphiné.

Car travel
Rental. Normal documentation, driving licence, credit cards at airports and most tourist centres.
Own car. National driving licence, green card recommended, nationality sticker. Snow chains best bought at supermarkets, but can also be hired from garages.
Speed limits. 130 kph (80 mph) on péage (toll) motorways, 100 kph (62 mph) on dual carriageways and non toll motorways, 80 kph (50 mph) on other roads.
Touring club de France (TCF). 6–8 rue Firmin-Gillot, 75015 Paris, tel (1) 532 22 15.
Road conditions. Inter service route, tel (1) 48 58 33 33.
Breakdown. Emergency telephones on péage every 2 km.

Unleaded petrol is not widely available in the French Alps. Tourist offices can provide a list of locations. Péage motorways are common and

represent the quickest way to get from the Channel ports to the Alps, costing about £30. Priority to the right at junctions.

Rail travel
This is less well developed for local journeys in France than, say, Switzerland, although the Train Grand Vitesse (TGV) from Paris is a fast and comfortable way to reach Lyon or Geneva. For Haute Savoie, the following stations are convenient – Annemasse, Thonon, Cluses, Sallanches/St Gervais, Annecy.

Maps
Michelin do excellent road maps, also the IGN maps are good at a scale of 1:250,000. No. 112 covers most of the French Alps. Walking and climbing maps at 1:25,000 are very detailed.

Medical
You might be eligible for emergency cover under form E111, check with British DHSS. Otherwise full travel insurance with skiing and mountaineering cover is recommended. Carte Neige is good for skiing, and the Club Alpin Français insurance good for general mountaineering.

Weather. General Paris Météo number (1) 45 55 91 88.
Snow reports. Paris Ski France (1) 42 66 64 28; Haute Savoie 79 35 00 50; Dauphiné-Isère 76 54 30 80.
Emergency. Fire dial 18, Police 17.

THE SWISS ALPS AT A GLANCE

Main Alpine ranges: Pennine, Bernese Oberland, Lepontine, Glarus, Adula, Rhaetian, Bernina.

Highest and best known summits: Dufourspitze (Monte Rosa) (4634 m/15,203 ft), Dom (4545 m/14,911 ft), Weisshorn (4506 m/14,783 ft), Matterhorn (4478 m/14,691 ft), Eiger (3975 m/13,041 ft), all in canton Valais.

Best known Alpine towns/resorts: Zermatt for the Matterhorn, Grindelwald for the Eiger, Verbier for skiing, St Moritz for money.

Main lakes: Geneva/Lac Leman (shared with France), Constance/Bodensee (shared with Germany), Neuchâtel, Maggiore, Lucerne (Vierwaldstattesee – Lake of the four cantons), Lake of Zürich.

Other physical features: Aletsch Glacier (Valais) 87 sq km (33.55 sq miles), rivers Rhine, Aar and Rhône.

Tourist Offices
London, Swiss Centre, New Coventry Street, London W1V 8EE, tel (071) 734 1921.

22. Briançon.

New York, Swiss Center, 608 Fifth Avenue, New York, NY 10020, tel (212) 757 5944.
San Francisco, 260 Stockton Street, San Francisco, CA 94108/5367, tel (415) 362 2260.

Embassies
British, Dufourstrasse 56, Zürich, tel (01) 47 15 20.
USA, Zolliker Strasse 141, Zürich. tel (01) 55 2566.

Visas

British passport holders, valid passport up to 90 days stay.

USA passport holders, valid passport up to 90 days stay.

Languages

French, German, Italian, Romansch, English widely spoken in tourist areas.

Currency

Swiss Francs, 100 centimes (£1 = 2.50 SFR; $1 = 1.5 SFR). Main banks 08.30 to 12.30, 13.30 to 16.30 weekdays. Railways stations can change cash or Eurocheques daily 06.30 to 21.00. Credit cards accepted in main tourist areas where signs displayed, but smaller businesses prefer cash. Passport required when cashing Traveller's Cheques or Eurocheques. Service charge/tipping is mostly included in prices, but porters get one or two francs per bag; 15% applies where not included.

Electricity

220 volt, 50 cycle AC; take a European plug adapter.

Accommodation

Swiss hotels are justifiably world famous. Not cheap, but good value. Local tourist offices can provide names of local families who let out rooms. Chalets and self-catering flats are best booked in advance through agencies at home – cheapest for groups and families. Anyone can sleep in youth hostels but under 25s have priority.

Air travel

Zürich airport has its own railway station, 10 minutes from the city centre. Geneva airport has a coach service every 20 minutes from the city centre. Basel airport has a coach service every 30 minutes to the city centre. Onward rail connections are extensive. A useful Swiss service is fly-luggage, whereby your main baggage can be checked in up to 24 hours in advance of the flight at main railway stations, to reappear at your flight destination.

Car travel

Rental. It is always best to get maximum insurance and collision damage waiver. Valid driving licence, held for one year, minimum age 21. Some agencies at railways stations. Credit card preferred.

Own car. Green card extension to your own policy is recommended, registration papers and national driving licence, nationality sticker, red warning triangle, motorway sticker. Snow chains may be required in winter, obtainable from petrol stations. Priority to the right, to uphill vehicles on mountain roads and postal buses.

Speed limits. Motorways 120 kph (74 mph), other roads 80 kph (50 mph), cars towing caravans 80 kph (50 mph) anywhere.

Automobile Club der Schweiz (ACS), Wasserwerkgasse 39, CH 3000 Berne 13, tel 031 224722. *Touring Club der Schweiz* (TCS), Rue Pierre Fatio 9, CH 121 Genève, tel 022 371212.

Breakdown. Call TCS on a motorway telephone or by dialling 140 on a public phone. Members of an affiliated service will not be charged for assistance.

Road conditions. Phone 163.

Rail travel

As efficient and punctual as the Swiss clocks. Regular hourly service in almost every direction. Reductions in the form of excursion tickets and Swiss holiday cards, regional holiday cards.

Maps

Swiss Touring club road map, 1:300,000. Detailed walking and ski maps are available 1:50,000 (LK Schweiz).

Medical

There is no state medical system and therefore no possible reciprocity with the UK National Health system. Comprehensive travel insurance is recommended, to include loss of baggage, personal effects and delay/cancellation. Be sure to have full winter sports coverage and mountaineering extensions, where appropriate, since a mountain rescue bill can run into thousands of pounds or dollars. The Swiss Rega helicopter rescue insurance provides additional cover.

Weather. Phone 162.
Snow reports. Phone 120 for snow and avalanche conditions.
Emergency. Phone 117 (police).

Generally, the Swiss Holiday card for periods of 4, 8, 15 days and one month gives unlimited travel on train bus and boat, with reductions for mountain railways.

THE ITALIAN ALPS AT A GLANCE

Main Alpine ranges: Graian, Ortler, Dolomites.

Highest and best known summits: Gran Paradiso (highest mountain solely in Italy; 4060 m/ 13,320 ft), Monte Rosa (Italian summit; 4618 m/ 15,151 ft), Marmolada (Dolomites; 3342 m/ 10,964 ft), Tre Cime di Lavaredo (Drei Zinnen; 2998 m/9836 ft), Mt Cervin (Matterhorn, Italian summit; 4477 m/14,688 ft), Pelmo (one of the first Dolomite peaks to be climbed; 3168 m/ 10,394 ft).

Best known Alpine towns/resorts: Aosta and Courmayeur for climbing and skiing, Val Gardena, Cervinia and Cortina D'Ampezzo for skiing.

Tourist Office
London, 1 Princes Street, W1R 8AY, tel (071) 839 6255.
New York, 630 Fifth Avenue, NY 10111, tel 245 4961.
San Francisco, St Francis Hotel, Suite 801, 360 Post Street, San Francisco, CA 94108, tel 39 25 266.

Embassies
British, Via 20 Settembre 80a, 00187 Rome, tel 475–5441.
USA, Via Vittorio Veneto, 119 Rome, tel 4674.

Visas
British passport holders, valid passport up to 90 days' stay.

23. *Lugano, Ticino.*

USA passport holders, valid passport up to 90 days' stay.

Languages
Italian; not much English spoken, even in resorts.

Currency
Lire, £1 = about 2350, $1 = about 1330 lire. Changes and banks will take Travellers and Eurocheques.

Electricity
220 volt, 50 cycle AC, take a European plug adapter. Occasional 125 volt outlets make it wise to ask.

Accommodation
Alpine accommodation varies. Hotels (albergo) are in five categories. Breakfast is generally not included, but 20% tax and service is often 'tutto compresso', included in the price. 'Pensioni' offer accommodation with families, 'Locanda' offer basic accommodation in inns, while apartments, as usual, offer the best rates for large groups who are able to book in advance. Christmas and Easter are fully booked in most ski resorts, so plan ahead.

Air travel

Milan International is the main Italian airport in striking distance of the Alps, with a 20-minute bus service to the city air terminal. It may also be just as convenient to fly to Innsbruck in Austria for access to the Dolomites in the eastern Italian Alps via the Brenner pass.

Car travel

Rental. Car hire is available at most international airports, minimum age 21–25, credit card advised to avoid huge cash deposits.

Own car. A Green card is advised, and you will need an International Driving permit or national licence, national sticker and red warning triangle.

Petrol coupons are available to give tourists reduced rates.

Speed limits are based on the engine size of the car (Italian 'machismo' perhaps?). In built up areas the limit is usually 50 kph (30 mph), while on the open road a 1300 cc car can travel 100 kph (62 mph) and 130 kph (80 mph) on motorways. Over 1300 cc engines can travel 110 kph (70 mph) on the open road, 140 kph (85 mph) on motorways. Motorways have tolls based on distance. Major road traffic has priority, a rule which is frequently ignored. One can only advise caution at all times.

Auto club D'Italia. (ACI) Via Marsala 8, Roma.

Breakdown. Dial 116 for assistance from the ACI. (English speaking assistance.)

Rail travel

This is available through the state network, one of the cheapest in Europe, but less extensive in the Alps than in the plains. The best Alpine services are north–south on the main international routes connecting with Switzerland. East–west services are less frequent and delays are not uncommon.

Maps

These are best acquired at news-stands and tourist offices. The ACI publish excellent free 1:200,000 road maps with a useful tourist gazette on the reverse. For detailed walking and climbing excursions, the 1:35,000 national park maps are excellent and informative.

Medical

Form E111 will entitle EEC nationals to free public health care in Italy. But it is wise to take out a general travel policy, with skiing and mountaineering extensions.

Weather and **Snow reports** can be obtained on the following numbers: Western Piedmont Aosta Valley (011) 5731, Dolomites (041) 993162, Central Alps, Lombardy plain (02) 67509. **Emergency** dial 113.

THE AUSTRIAN ALPS AT A GLANCE

Main Alpine ranges: Ötztal, Stubai, Carnic, Zillertal, Tauern (Hohe and Niedere), Vorarlberg, Karwendel, Lechtaler, Kitzbüheler.

Highest and best known summits: Gross Glockner (3797 m/12,457 ft).

Best known Alpine towns/resorts: St Anton for skiing, Hahnenkamm (The Streif) at Kitzbühel for the Downhill race.

Tourist Offices

London, 30 St George Street, London W1R 0AH, tel (071) 629 0461
New York, 500 Fifth Avenue, Suite 2009–2022, NY 10010, tel (212) 944 6880.
Los Angeles 11601, Suite 2480, Willshire Boulevard, Los Angeles, CA 90025 tel (213) 477 3332.

Embassies

British, Reisnerstrasse 40, 1030 Vienna, tel (0222) 731575.
USA, Boltzmanngasse 16, 1090 Vienna, tel (0222) 346611.

Visas

British passport holders, valid passport up to 90 days' stay.
USA passport holders, no visa required.

Languages

German is the national language, but English is widely spoken in the tourist areas.

Currency

Austrian Schilling, 100 Gröschen. Money can be changed in many places, credit cards and Eurocheques are widely used. Banks open weekdays 0745 to 1230, 1430 to 1600. £1 = about 22 AS, $1 = about 13 AS.

Electricity

220 volt, 50 cycle AC; take a European plug adapter.

Accommodation

This is good and varied, with a strong tradition of 'gemütlichkeit', varying from first class hotels to simple Alpine hostels. Tirolean farmhouses can be cheap and fun as a base for a walking holiday or the odd night on the road. Mountain huts are available on many of the higher walking routes, but ask in the valleys about whether they have a guardian who does the cooking or whether you need to get a key and fend for yourself.

Air travel

Munich International and Salzburg are the most convenient for the mountains of Austria. Munich is about two hours by road from the Tirol.

Car travel

Rental. Credit cards are best, for the over 21s with a driving licence. Cheaper rates are available for those booking in advance.
Own car. The normal licence and registration documents, warning triangle and international sticker. Snow tyres and chains are necessary in winter, the latter can be hired from the Austrian auto club. Tolls are levied on some high level roads, e.g. the Grossglocknerstrasse, Brenner motorway etc.
Speed limits. Motorways 130 kph (80 mph), other roads 100 kph (62 mph), towns 50 kph (30 mph).

Auto club and Breakdown. ÖAMTC tel (05222) 441154, ARBO (05222) 45123.

Rail travel

The Austria ticket (16 days) for around 1400 AS is a good bargain if you wish to make a number of train journeys.

Maps

Special maps for hikers are available from tourist offices. The Kompass series covers the main mountain areas.

Medical

Personal insurance with skiing and mountain extensions are recommended, although a limited free emergency service is available.

Weather. Phone 1566.
Snow reports. Vienna, Lower Austria 1583, Salzburg, Upper Austria 1584 (avalanche warning 1588), Tirol Vorarlberg 1585 (avalanche warning 1588).
Emergency. Mountain rescue 194, police 133, ambulance 144.

THE GERMAN ALPS AT A GLANCE

Main Alpine ranges: Bavarian Alps, Karwendel.

Highest and best known summits: Zugspitze (highest at 2966 m/9731 ft), Watzmann (2713 m/8901 ft).

Best known Alpine towns/resorts: Garmisch Partenkirchen for World Cup skiing, Berchtesgaden for skiing and summer walking.

Other physical features: The lake at Bodensee/Constance, Neuschwanstein castle, German Alpine road.

Tourist Offices
London, Nightingale House, 65 Curzon Street, London W1Y 7PE, tel (071) 495 3990.
New York 747 Third Avenue, 33rd floor, NY 10017, tel (212) 308 3300.
Los Angeles, 444 South Flower St, Suite 2230, Los Angeles CA 90071, tel (213) 688 7332.

Embassies
British, Consulate General of the UK, Amalienstrasse 62, 8000 Munich 40, tel (089) 394015.
USA, Consulate General, Königin Strasse 5, 8000 Munich 22, tel (089) 23011.

Visas
British passport holders, valid passport.
USA passport holders, no visa required with valid passport up to 90 days' stay.

Languages
German, but English quite widely spoken in tourist areas.

Currency
German Mark (DM), £1 = about 3.2 DM, $1 = about 1.8 DM. Credit cards, Travellers Cheques and Eurocheques all useful.

Electricity
220 volt, 50 cycle AC; take a European plug adapter.

Accommodation
Aside from the normal high quality hotels in Alpine resorts, farm holidays and accommodation in castle hotels and stately homes offer an attractive alternative. Self-catering holiday villages, flats and bungalows are also available. Obtain details from tourist offices well in advance.

Air travel
Munich and Salzburg in Austria are the most convenient for the German Alpine resorts.

Car travel
Rental. Booking offices are available at all main airports, city centres, and railway stations.
Own car. Normal European documentation applies, International Driving Permit is required unless USA driving licence is accompanied by a German translation. A Green Card is recommended, but temporary cover can be taken out at the border.
Speed limits. 130 kph (80 mph) on motorways (tollfree), 100 kph (62 mph) on other roads, 50 kph (30 mph) in town. Trailers and caravans 80 kph (50 mph) outside towns.
Auto Club and Breakdown. ADAC provide service free, except for cost of materials. Ask for 'Strassenwachthilfe' (road service assistance).

Rail travel
Savings can be made on normal fares with a variety of concessions for children, Saver tickets, Super Savers and Rail Rover tickets, young persons, senior citizens and family Railcards.

Maps
Topographisch Carte, 1:25,000, 1:50,000.

Medical
Reciprocal arrangements through form E111, but holiday and travel insurance recommended.

Weather. Phone 1164.
Snow reports. Phone (089) 76 76 26 86.
Emergency. Phone 110.

THE YUGOSLAV ALPS AT A GLANCE

Main Alpine ranges: Julian

Highest and best known summits: Triglav (2864 m/9396 ft).

Best known Alpine towns/resorts: Kranjska Gora and Bohinj for skiing, Bled for its magical lake and mountain views.

Tourist Offices
London, 143 Regent Street, London W1, tel (071) 734 5243.
New York, Suite 210, Rockefeller Center, 630 Fifth Avenue, NY 10020, tel (212) 2757 2801.

Embassies
British, Generala Zdanova 46, Belgrade, tel 645 055.
USA, Kneza Milosa 50, Belgrade, tel 645 655.

Visas
British passport holders, valid passport up to 90-day stay.

USA passport holders, automatic visa on arrival.

Languages
Unbelievably complicated. Two alphabets, and numerous languages: Serbo-Croatian, Slovenian, Macedonian, Albanian, Turkish, Romanian, to name but a few. Whatever your skills, they are likely to be useless. Loud English is increasingly used in tourist areas; German can be useful as a back-up in and around the Julian Alps region.

Currency
The Yugoslav new dinar (= 100 old dinars, in which prices are sometimes quoted). £1 = 9400 dinar, $1 = 5400 dinar. Banks are open 0800 to 1900, with a lunch break. Credit cards are beginning to be used, but cash and Travellers Cheques are safer. Do not change too much, as Dinars cannot be changed back before leaving and are useless outside the country.

Electricity
220 volt, 50 cycle AC; take a European plug adapter.

Accommodation
This comprises the normal range of hotels, motels, pensions apartments and private rooms with families. Additionally some ski resorts have tourist villages.

Air travel
Ljubljana in the north is the most convenient for the Alps.

Car travel
Rental. Credit cards, 12-hour 'day' rates vary tremendously in most major tourist centres.
Own car. The normal documents, licence and registration, nationality sticker and Green Card are recommended (the Yugoslav supplement can add quite a bit to the standard Green Card cost). Roads are fair except minor roads which can be appalling, especially in the mountains which can be full of surprises, so be prepared for an adventure. Petrol coupons offer a slight reduction in the cost of petrol.

24. *Ski Mountaineer, Haute Route France.*

Speed limits. 120 kph (75 mph) on motorways, 100 kph (62 mph) on main roads, 80 kph (50 mph) on secondary roads, 60 kph (40 mph) in town.
Auto club and Breakdown. For AMSJ assistance 0800 to 1900 dial 987.

Rail travel
This is limited in the Alpine areas.

Maps
Often free from tourist offices.

Medical
Independent insurance is recommended, but residents of Great Britain are entitled to reciprocal national health care, by obtaining form E111 in advance of departure.

Weather. It is best to ask at tourist offices.
Emergency. Phone 94 (coin needed).

CHAPTER SEVEN

Photography in the Alps

[The] *great cathedrals of the earth, with their gates of rock, pavements of clouds, choirs of stream and stone, altars of snow, and vaults of purple traversed by continual stars.*
– Ruskin.
Take only photographs, leave only tracks.

Given the unique degree to which Alpine landscapes have terrified, inspired and acted as a magnet for travellers from all over the world, it is hardly surprising that you too will want to record your own Alpine experiences on film.

PHOTOGRAPHERS AS EXPLORERS

Some of the very first and most daring explorers of high ground in the Alps were painters, commissioned by the wealthy or by institutions to bring back stunning images of the Alps. For many people these were the first glimpses ever seen of this strange and forbidding part of the earth.

Later, photographers took over as the image makers, although by today's standards their equipment was a long way from that of the snapshooter. In these early days, pioneers of the trade would walk all day in search of the right combination of foreground, background, light and shade, carrying an enormous weight of equipment. In 1861, French photographer Bisson needed 25 porters to get his photographic equipment to the summit of Mont Blanc. This included a large tripod and enormous box camera, as well as fragile glass plates to be coated with emulsion just before the moment of exposure, and were often developed immediately afterwards.

Whereas the most commonly used negative size today is that of the 35 mm camera, the negatives of the pioneers would often measure up to 10 × 12 inches. Because of their lack of technical advantages, taking a good photograph would often be the result of a vocational day's work with porters and paraphernalia. But the prints of the early photographers are not only of historical interest. They measure up favourably against the work of the best of today's mountain photographers. This is because the massive negative size encourages minimal intrusion of grain into the final image. Also the fact that a shot took so long to set up meant that they waited until everything was right before releasing the shutter.

Unfortunately all the modern technology in the world, autofocus, motordrives, fast film, coated lenses, trick filters and talking cameras can still not guarantee anything more than a mediocre photograph today, whether it be at sea level on the beach or on the ski slopes. Good images from the mountains still, and always will, require infinite patience, a good sense of composition, and quite frequently a good pair of legs to get you to the places other tourists do not reach.

Photographic magazines are always extolling the virtues of the very latest camera which will make your holiday photography easy. Ask a professional, and he or she will tell you that all you need is one camera which you have used regularly and are comfortable with. Once you have found it, stick to it and concentrate on your techniques. Mostly it is the photographer, not the camera, who makes the best pictures.

BASIC EQUIPMENT

A 35 mm single lens reflex camera is the best compromise of weight, adaptability and quality. If you decide to pursue photography as a hobby, interchangeable lenses and attachments can be built on to the basic body bit by bit. Simple mechanical cameras with mechanical shutters are better in the mountains than cameras in which everything works by batteries. These always let you down when you most need them.

Lenses

The best all-purpose lens is the 28 mm or 35 mm lens which gives a fairly wide angle of view and reasonable depth of field, within which everything is in focus. The 50 mm lens is often described as the lens which most nearly corresponds to the natural perspective seen by the human eye, but I find it neither telephoto nor wide angle enough to be much use as a 'standard lens'.

The 105 mm and 135 mm lenses are very useful as a medium telephoto lens while not being too heavy nor having too little depth of field. Lenses of 200 mm, 300 mm and over are excellent for creating tightly cropped views of distant scenes, animals, or walkers on a ridge, but are often too heavy to be carried conveniently on the camera. Thus they are rarely to hand when quickly needed, and mostly require a slow shutter speed

and tripod to obtain an image without camera shake.

Zoom lenses used to be a lot less satisfactory than prime (fixed focal length) lenses, but for most cases a good zoom is now indistinguishable from a prime lens. You can save weight by taking a zoom with you, but they can lead to a great deal of wasted film because of framing indecision.

Basic filters

Whatever lenses you use, a skylight filter should be left on the camera at all times. This cuts out haze and a little of the blue light so prevalent at high altitude, as well as protecting the lens. Other basic filters I carry are a polarizing filter and a 25A deep red filter.

The polarizer is most effective at 90 degrees to the sun, when it will darken the blue sky, penetrate haze, enhance bright colours and suppress reflections. Open your lens aperture by one and a half stops to allow for the filter, e.g. from f11/16 to f8. The deep red filter needs a three stop increase in exposure (e.g. f16 to f5.6). It also darkens blue sky to black, whitens clouds, and penetrates haze, producing dramatic effects in black and white photography.

Best compromise

I have found the best compromise for the committed mountain photographer is to have two identical or similar camera bodies, one loaded with colour, one with black and white film. Lenses can be interchanged. If one is damaged, the other is always available as a spare. Smaller automatic cameras are fine for snaps, but lenses cannot be exchanged, filters are not always available and the extent of manual control, which is essential for a good result rather than a machine-induced fluke, is limited.

Keep it simple. My basic equipment comprises two Nikon FE2 camera bodies, 35 mm and 105 mm lenses with skylight filters, a polarizer and 25A red filter. One reason for minimizing on

25. *Photographer on the move* (over the page).

lenses is that you need only carry one size of filter. Cameras can easily be carried around your neck or in specially designed 'camera care' type pouches on the waist band of a backpack.

Exposure

Automatic cameras and cameras with exposure meters are very useful if the sun is coming from behind you and the subject matter is of 'average' reflectivity, which manufacturers call 18 per cent grey. Most subjects are not that obliging. If you are pointing your camera at the sun, at a snowslope or at a dark forest of pines, your 'automatic' exposure meter will give an inaccurate result.

Two things have to be considered. First, how much light is falling on the subject from behind the camera: the incident light? Second, how much light is being reflected from the subject: the reflected light? As a general rule, the right setting will be achieved if you can find an average subject lit with the same light as your subject. Take a reading from this and use it as a guide for the main picture. This is explained in more detail below when I discuss photography on the snow.

Try to select subjects without too much difference between light and dark areas, since the exposure range of most films will not be able to record all the details in highlight or shade. As a general rule, when using negative (print film), err on the side of overexposure (give the film plenty of light) so that there is detail in the shadows. With colour transparency film (slides) concentrate on the highlights, the brightest areas. Err on the side of underexposure. Do not allow the highlights to 'burn out' because of too much light reaching the film.

Other formats

Professional landscape photographers still carry large format cameras into the mountains, as did their forebears, since this is still the best way to

27. *Tripod for landscapes.*

obtain top quality for maximum enlargement. Medium format cameras such as the Hasselblad offer a good compromise of quality and portability. But where action photography is required, the 35 mm SLR camera is still the best. While producing remarkable results for their size and portability, 110 and disc cameras are great for snaps, but not much else.

Tripod for landscapes

One of the simplest ways to improve the quality of your landscapes is to use a tripod for any static subject. Not only does this eliminate the possibility of camera shake – more likely than you think at altitude when your heart is pumping with the exertion of a climb – but also it will enable you to use a slow shutter speed for maximum depth of field to keep everything in focus.

A variety of filters can attempt to improve the conditions as you find them. But none can really improve on what God can do on a good day. One

26. *Wood and stone, Sion castle* (previous page).

of the tenets of landscape photography is to represent the landscape as it is rather than as a manipulated image of composite filters and tricks. Filters have their place, as in a graduated filter for darkening a part of the sky too bright to register on film, but as a general rule they are an irrelevance to landscape photography.

IN SEARCH OF THE ENDURING LANDSCAPE

I cannot tell you what to photograph any more than I could tell you where to stand and which way to look. But some general guidelines may help to obtain some better than average images.

From the plane

Your first chance of good Alpine views may occur even before you arrive on your inward flight. Having worked out the geography of your approach, secure a window seat. Set your shutter speed to at least 1/500th of a second, cut out reflections with a sweater or jacket against the window and over your head. Set the focus at infinity, but avoid letting the camera touch the window. You may have some surprising results even before you land.

The magic hours

The 'magic hours' of dawn and dusk often produce the most interesting light in the mountains, but this requires a very early start or missing out on dinner. You have to be a committed photographer to catch this light, but it is usually worth it, particularly in winter when the only colour is white snow. In the middle of the day, overhead light gives little drama to the mountains, whereas a low morning or evening light etches character into any scene.

Heavy weather drama

Bad weather produces the most dramatic scenes and lighting so, whatever the weather, keep your camera handy, wrapped if necessary in a plastic bag. A slow shutter speed say 1/30th of a second will blur falling snow or rain for an epic photograph. But learn to work quickly, since the clouds change everything in seconds and mountains really do go away, not to reappear for days. You rarely get a second chance in the Alps.

Work for the angle

When on climbing, walking and skiing trips, try and get ahead or to the side of the action for the best angles. Too many shots of these sports just show backs of heads and bottoms. Use a fast shutter speed, say 1/500th of a second, for action. It is best to pre-focus on a spot and wait for the action to come to you.

In search of inspiration

Study magazines and brochures of your favourite mountain sports. Try and work out what it is you like about the photographs which most impress you. With practice you can work out lenses, filters, shutter speeds and aperture stop just by looking at the photograph. When you are in the mountains, think in terms of photographic opportunities. You will learn to feel them developing. You can take photographs in your head, practising even without a camera.

For pure landscape, never pass up a chance to see exhibitions of Alpine paintings, modern and ancient. Admittedly the painters can always place a chalet or a peak where they will, but the proportions, the perspectives and the sense of drama will add to your visual vocabulary and spark off new ideas and opportunities.

Two books on Alpine painting which contain stimulating records of Alpine art are: *Faszination Bergmalerei*, Schaer Verlag, Thun.
This is a summary of the great Alpine painters, including those from non-Alpine nations, e.g. Turner. It contains some superb work, also from the modern school. It has tips on how to be your own Alpine painter, as well as actual grid references in the Grindelwald area of where the best places are for painting landscapes and finding summer flowers, leaving no excuses for not coming back with a special picture!

Les Alps Vues par Les Peintres, Maurice Jean-Petit-Matile.
A wonderful record of Alpine painting through the years, starting with Turner. The cover is a spectacular view of Mont Blanc at sunrise, that 'magic hour' again.

SNOW AND SKI PHOTOGRAPHY

The mountain environment can be as hostile as any to the making of good pictures. Temperatures down to −35°C, howling winds, frozen hands, dead batteries, altitude, snapping film, static electricity, and a background which is about as far away from 18 per cent grey as it could be – these are just some of the problems which the Alpine photographer may encounter.

Amateur or professional, holidays are a great photographic opportunity. Compared to the cost of the trip, the cost of film is negligible. It's only fair to yourself to bring home a good set of pictures, particularly from skiing trips, where bright sun and highly reflective snow give many good picture opportunities.

Yet so many people come home from ski trips with little more than memories. You had great snow and the sun always shone, but all the pictures show are the shadowy ghosts of headless skiers, knee deep in grey snow . . . and then come the excuses. 'Somebody pushed me just as I released the shutter . . . the Eiger is behind my thumb' . . . etc.

Unfortunately it is more likely to be the photographer who is to blame and not the equipment. So here are some hot tips for cold pictures, to put the white back into your snow, the blue back into the sky and those sparkling eyes back into your snow photography . . .

Think before you shoot

The real difference between professional and amateur is that, on the whole, professionals think about their photography. Consciously or unconsciously, they are always asking the question 'Why am I taking this shot?'

The result is that the picture works. Professionals know and care for their equipment like old friends. Like old friends, their equipment can be relied on. Good photography is really about being in control of the result; that's how they stay in business. But non-professionals, understandably, have less time to practise.

Before leaving home

First check your camera. Clean it, put in new batteries, run a short roll of film through and check the results. Decide what equipment you want to take to the slopes. Most importantly, keep gear to a minimum. Otherwise it will be left in the hotel. Get organized and you are halfway down the slope towards good ski photography.

It may be far better to carry just one compact camera, than a backpack full of gear which you will not have the time to use. Admittedly, when on a professional assignment, I would carry at least two camera bodies, one for colour and one for black and white, a selection of lenses, and maybe a spare body too. But then I'm not on holiday, you are! So do not overburden yourself.

Film

Decide how much film you will probably use, then take twice as much. You can always bring it home again. Locally they are almost always out of the film you want, and what is left is expensive or out of date. I always take my camera gear as hand luggage; it is then safe from theft or breakage *en route*. But not safe, perhaps, from airport X-rays . . .

Personally I do no trust X-ray machines. I always ask for a hand search and have all my film ready to be opened and examined, I generally go through the departure gate 30 minutes early just for this reason! Repeated exposure to X-rays, says Kodak, is the problem. If you prefer a quiet life, take the risk. But if you want to be in total control of your results from start to finish, then

28. Heavy weather, Haute Route, France.

the answer must be obvious. With the increase of terrorism, the chances of being allowed to have your baggage hand-searched are small. The best solution would seem to be to place your film with your checked baggage.

I always use the slowest film possible for the lighting conditions. Snowscenes have a lot of reflected light, which means you can use Kodachrome 25 or 64. If you want to shoot action, and have some depth of field in the background, you will need 200 ASA or even 400 ASA film. Fujichrome film gives bright colours, with clean whites for snow and is one of my favourites in the mountains. If your final aim is to have photographs published in magazines, always use transparencies for colour, and print film for black and white.

On the snow

On the snow, start with looking after yourself. You will never take good pictures if you are not comfortable and warm, especially your hands. It might help to use a very thin second glove under your ski glove, so you can use the camera and still keep warm.

Carry your camera where it is easily accessible and can be kept warm and dry if you fall. If the camera gets cold, the batteries may fail even if new, and if your camera is fully automatic, that's the end of photography until you can warm it up again. If you anticipate very cold conditions, get your camera winterized so that the oil does not freeze.

Batteries in motordrives can also suffer. Film becomes brittle when cold and can snap on winding. Also, dry mountain air is highly charged with static electricity. This can cause sparks inside the camera body which will blemish the film. Wind and re-wind slowly by hand.

Snow exposure

Exposure is a common problem on the snow.

Being calibrated to an average grey, most metering will tend to underexpose snow pictures. The meter thinks there is more light available than there actually is. There are a number of ways around this problem.

You could do worse than to rely on the manufacturers' recommendations for snow scenes. Or you can fill the frame of a TTL (through the lens metering) camera with a grey or neutrally coloured anorak, a tanned face, or the back of your hand and then lock on this reading for the general scene. If you carry a meter, take an incident light reading, which will be unaffected by the glare of a predominantly white scene. All of these methods will be more accurate than blindly relying on TTL metering.

Then set your camera manually. Those with automatic cameras may have to lock the exposure, or fool the meter by adjusting the exposure compensation dial to '+2'. Alternatively you can adjust the ASA rating to tell the camera that it is loaded with film one stop slower than it actually carries i.e. 100 ASA instead of 200 ASA.

These dodges only apply when the scene is dominated by snow. If you are taking a 'full frame' close-up, then go back to the normal TTL metering. For further insurance, bracket your exposures to either side of the indicated reading. Most professionals do this whenever the shot is important. Another safeguard is to use colour negative film rather than transparency. An exposure which is one stop out can still be adequately printed back home, whereas the smaller latitude of transparency film is such that the shot may be lost because of inaccurate exposure.

Many professionals argue that photography begins, not ends, when the shutter is released. By all means shoot more film, but show less. Select the best from your ski pictures and have them enlarged. Better by far to show ten really good shots than three rolls of mediocrity. And if you get some really good ones, put them on the wall.

CHAPTER EIGHT

The Alps by Train

The dusty and deafening railroad rush.
— Mark Twain, *A Tramp Abroad.*

Getting to the Alps by train is easy and quick with the French TGV from Paris to Grenoble, Geneva, Lyon, Berne and Lausanne, as well as direct services from London Victoria through to Munich, Vienna, etc.

In Europe, the Inter-Rail card is valid for the under 26s for one month's unlimited travel. Current price in UK (1989) is £145. For visitors originating outside Europe, the Eurailpass offers discounted first-class transport in all Alpine countries except Yugoslavia, while the Eurail Youth pass is available for the under 26s. In the USA both the Eurailpass and the Eurail Youth pass must be purchased before departure.

The Alpine countries are all serviced by train networks to varying degrees of efficiency. In general terms Switzerland has the only service which will get you just about anywhere in the Alps, including some place not accessible by car.

In London, make enquiries at the Victoria Station European Travel Centre.

THE FRENCH ALPS BY TRAIN

Unlike Switzerland, the French Alpine train system is good for getting into the Alps, but less convenient for going from place to place. Memorable transalpine journeys are the Alpazur from Geneva to Nice, or the shorter sampler of Grenoble to Veynes-Devoluy. Good views of Mont Aiguille and the Vercors ramparts can be had from the train.

The France Vacances pass rail-rover tickets offer unlimited rail travel on any 4 days within 15 days or on any 9 days during a period of one month in first or second class. Under 26s qualify for up to 50 per cent reduction on rail travel with a Carte Jeune rail card, depending on the date of travel.

Air France Rail is a bargain price ticket for a combination of air and train travel to any of 3000 stations in France. This can also be combined with a 15-day France Vacances pass.

Two memorable French Alpine train journeys in the Mont Blanc region are the train to Montenvers overlooking the Mer de Glace, and the Mont Blanc Tramway to the Nid D'Aigle overlooking the Glacier de Bionassay.

Train to Montenvers. Catch this rack railway behind the Chamonix railway station, 45 minutes to the summit of Montenvers. The train was inaugurated in 1908, having been the destination of a mule track since 1802, originally popularized by the Englishmen Windham and Pocock in 1741 who dubbed the Mont Maudit area 'full of cursed mountains and their bewitched glaciers'.

Despite this the Montenvers is a pleasant sunny spot to spend a day, with a magnificent panorama of the Mer de Glace, the monolithic Drus, Aiguille Verte, Grande Jorasses and many other famous peaks. An orientation table assists identification. In winter the Mer de Glace is a flat white snow motorway leading from the Aiguille du Midi to Chamonix. In summer the glacier is bare, honeycombed with myriad crevasses, which make an interesting playground for trainee mountaineers. There is an hotel and restaurants, an ice grotto, rebuilt every summer, as well as an Alpine zoo with chamois, mouflons, marmottes, lynx and birds of prey.

The Mont Blanc Tramway (TMB) runs in summer only, eight times a day, to the Nid D'Aigle (Eagle's Nest) at 2386 m (7828 ft). The original plan was to take this tramway right to the summit of Europe's highest mountain, but we can be thankful that nature intervened to make construction just too difficult beyond the Eagle's Nest. Not surprisingly, superb views of the summit of Mont Blanc are to be seen as the train climbs via Col de Voza (winter skiing) and to the Nid. The TMB can be caught from St Gervais or by cable car from Priarion above Les Houches in the Chamonix valley.

At the terminus there is a snack kiosk, and a one-hour walk to the moraine of the Bionassay glacier, whence further views are available of spectacular avalanches off the Aiguille de Bionassay, the Aiguille du Goûter, and over the Sallanches valley.

The Nid D'Aigle is the starting point for many walks in the area, including the ascent of Mont Blanc via the Goûter ridge and hut. Allow three hours return from St Gervais to the Nid.

In the Dauphiné Alps, the **Chemin de Fer de La Mure** has just celebrated its centenary as one of the most spectacular Alpine train rides, a 19-km (12-mile) narrow gauge. Now it runs on electric power, taking two hours between St Georges de Commiers and La Mure, through tunnels, over bridges and viaducts, crossing the gorges of the Drac. Far below the Drac dams can be seen as

well as magnificent views of the Vercors, in the shape of Mont Aiguille, L'Obiou and L'Oisanas. This is a day or half-day outing from Grenoble. Several trips run each week from May to October, with narration and photo stops. For details ask at Grenoble tourist office.

THE SWISS ALPS BY TRAIN

This little subject would merit a book in itself. In fact whole books have been written about small areas of the extensive Swiss mountain railway system. Recommended for the Bernese Oberland is the book by Maureen G. Cooling, *Ticket to the Top*.

Best rail access from the UK to Switzerland is either by TGV through France from Paris to Geneva, or direct to Bern, Basel, Lausanne or Zürich.

The Swiss Holiday card is one of the most efficient and cost-saving ways to travel around Switzerland, by train, bus or boat. For occasional rail travellers wanting a break from the road, half-fare season tickets are useful and entitle you to first or second class travel for return journeys on rail, bus or boat and funiculars. Regional Holiday Season Tickets are available in 9 Swiss regions, valid for a 15-day period, and offer free travel for 5 days of your choice, half price for the remaining 10 days, and 7 days unlimited travel in the Lugano/Locarno Swiss/Italian lake district.

Nostalgia dies hard, nowhere harder than in Switzerland where the *Orient Express* rears its stately head in the form of 19 restored railway carriages from the 1926–9 period, fitted out by well-known art deco artists. The Istanbul–Orient express is popular for incentive trips by Swiss and foreign participants. Apart from the main journey, day trips such as the Gotthard Pullman Express to Lugano are available to chartering groups.

29. *View from the Nid D'Aigle to the glacier de Bionassay, Chamonix.*

The Rhaetian railway. The construction of the Rhaetian railway at the turn of the century cut the journey time from Chur to St Moritz from 16 hours by horse and cart to four hours by train. In its 1930s heyday, the Rhaetian railway created the Engadine Express, to connect with luxury trains from London and Paris, with the then very latest in luxury transport – Pullman cars, sleeping cars and dining cars. More recently the 'Glacier Express' has become one of the most famous trains of the Alps, a route by which 200,000 holidaymakers a year take a unique view of the Swiss Alps on their journey from St Moritz and Zermatt.

The Engadine Express connects St Moritz with Landeck, Innsbruck, Salzburg and Vienna through the beautiful Engadine valley, at 2000 m (6500 ft) one of the highest valleys in the Alps, whose beauty is attested to by writers, poets and painters of ancient and modern times. The route

30. *Rhaetian railway, Switzerland, traditional costumes.*

takes you past the castle of Tarasp overlooking Scuol and passes close by the Swiss National Park, one of Europe's largest nature reserves.

The Bernina Express is the only railway in Switzerland which crosses the Alps without tunnelling. So none of those delicious views will be snatched away just as you are taking the lens cap off the camera. Through the snow-peaked Bernina mountains the 2400 m (7874 ft) summit pass is reached. Here summer lasts a mere four months, but makes up for it in the splendour of its flowers at the Alpine garden at Alp Grum, a popular stopoff point along the way. The train descends some 1800 m (6000 ft) to palm-fringed Tirano at the far end, with connections to Como and Milan, as well as further train journeys through the Italian Alps.

The **Glacier Express** was used for the first time in 1928 as a nostalgic trip connecting St Moritz with Zermatt, the Bernina to the Valais, via the 6-km (4-mile) Albula tunnel, the highest in the Alps. It may be 'the world's slowest express train', but despite that it still leaves Zermatt punctually every morning at 10.10 am, taking $7\frac{1}{2}$ hours through 91 tunnels and 291 bridges to St Moritz. Meals are available in the dining car. The trip is popular, so reserve well in advance.

Highlights along the way are the wild Schyn gorge and the castled valley of Domleschg, through the Rhine gorge to the Graubünden highland. Ilanz is the first town of the Rhine, shortly after which you pass Disentis and its famous monastery, whence the famous climbing monk Placidus à Spescha made many of his first ascents and climbing excursions.

Now into the pass region the train climbs to the Oberalp pass at 2033 m (6670 ft), thence

31. The Alps by train: Mürren, accessible by train, with views of the Eiger, Mönch and Jungfrau.

down towards Andermatt. The village of Gletch lies in severe scenery near the spectacular Rhône glacier. The track winds onwards along the vineyards of the Rhône valley before turning up to Täsch and Zermatt, the final destination. In eight or so hours high-level Switzerland has been condensed into a nutshell.

From Zermatt, the Gornergrat railway will take you up to the famous belvedere where, to the whirr of a thousand motordriven cameras, stands the world's best known peak, the Matterhorn. Here there is walking enough for weeks in summer, skiing in winter and of course climbing on the Matterhorn itelf.

Also worth the ticket is the new train trip on an old theme – the **William Tell Express** from Lucerne in central Switzerland to Locarno in the

sunny Ticino district. The one-way trip takes a day.

Last but not least of the selected Swiss mountain railway journeys (just a few of many) is the **Jungfrau Express** to the Jungfraujoch in the Bernese Oberland. Accessible from Interlaken, Kleine Scheidegg above Wengen and Grindelwald is the departure point for the Jungfraujoch train. Another hour will get you to the top. Wengen and Grindelwald are, of course, famous as winter ski resorts and summer climbing centres.

Looking at the Eiger and Mönch from Kleine Scheidegg, it is hard to imagine the sheer audacity of the mind – belonging to Friedrich Seiler – who conceived the idea of digging a $4\frac{1}{2}$-mile tunnel through the rock of one of the world's great north faces, just for tourism. But there it is. Half way up, at the Eigerwand station, you can look out of an observation window smack in the middle of the Eiger North Face.

At the Jungfraujoch there is a new 700-person restaurant, an ice palace and a museum of glaciology as well as the even stranger Sphinx observatory. The huddle of buildings resembles a 1920s artist's impression of a space station. Reached by a lift rising a further 118 m (129 yds) from the station the observatory (3454 m/11,332 ft) overlooks the Grosse Aletsch Glacier and the Konkordiaplatz where four glaciers meet.

When conditions are right there is off piste skiing on the glacier and the Obermönch hut can be reached in half an hour. Sledge dogs also operate in the summer months. In more senses than one the Jungfraujoch railway is one of the high spots of any Alpine journey.

THE ITALIAN ALPS BY TRAIN

Although train is a good way to approach the Italian Alps, the Aosta valley and the Dolomites, the most important and frequent routes are

32. Matterhorn and Gornergrat railway.

largely north–south, transalpine. Since the maximum benefit of Alpine travel is obtained by traversing rather than crossing, car travel is preferred for those who want to cover a lot of ground.

However the Tirano–Colico–Bergamo–Brescia–Edolo round trip with a gap between Edolo and Brescia is a possibility, covering the Valtelline, shores of Lake Como, through the Alpi Orobie.

Also attractive is the link between Brig, Domodossala, Locarno and Lugano. Lugano can be almost tropical in summer, and is the starting point for two funiculars which give rapid entry to the hills. These are to the Monte San Salvatore and Monte Bré. Here restaurants can be found with picturesque views from this lovely hill town to the Lake of Lugano. Walking around the area will considerably enhance the trip, especially to Gandria down at lake level again, whence a boat can be taken back to Lugano.

From Courmayeur a pleasant train trip can be made down the Aosta valley, close by the Gran Paradiso National Park.

A Dolomites train traverse goes west–east from Males Venosta through the Venosta valley to Merano, south-east to Bolzano (Bozen), north-east to Bressanone (Brixen), north-east through the beautiful Val Pusteria, to Brunico and Dobbiaco, crossing into Austria for the last 25 km or so to Lienz.

THE GERMAN ALPS BY TRAIN

For independent holiday-makers German Rail has two bargain fares, with reductions for accompanying adults and children aged 4–11. *Leisure Returns* are available from London to any Bavarian resort, while the *ten-day super saver* offers substantial savings for families with children. Both new fares can be combined with *Regional Rail Rovers* which give ten days' unlimited travel on German Rail within specified holiday regions. Current prices should be checked with the tourist office.

The cog railway up the Zugspitze on the Bavarian Zugspitzbahn is the most famous German Alpine railway, and is reached from Garmisch Partenkirchen (Zugspitzbahn station) to the Schneefernerhaus at 2645 m (8678 ft). There are hourly departures in both directions, but you should allow at least half a day for the round-trip excursion. Take some extra warm clothing whatever the weather down in Garmisch.

The journey is by electric rack railway to the tree-lined lake Eibsee. Eibsee can also be reached by car, and the train boarded there. A 4.5-km (2.7-mile) tunnel through the rock brings the journey to an end. The train is used summer and winter for skiers in a long November to May season. At the summit station there is a restaurant and further cable car to Zugspitzgipfel at 2966 m (9731 ft). There is not a great deal to do at the top, but the views are magnificent. An alternative is a cable car from the Austrian side or from Eibsee.

Some 100 km (60 miles) to the south-east of Munich lies the summit of Wendelstein, accessible also by mountain railway. Although not of great altitude, the 1800-m (5900-ft) summit is the site of Bavaria's oldest weather observatory, with panoramic views over southern Bavaria.

THE AUSTRIAN ALPS BY TRAIN

From London there are two main rail services from Victoria station, connecting with through services from Ostend. The daytime service connects with on the Ostend–Vienna Express via Passau for the Danube valley, Graz and Vienna. The afternoon service connects with the overnight service from Ostend to Salzburg, with connections in Ulm for Bregenz, in Munich for Mittenwald and Kufstein frontiers.

Austria too is well served for railway travellers, both for those who just wish to travel from A to B, as well as those who are railway buffs and enjoy the experience of travelling on a train just for the sake of it.

Of general application is the 'Go as you please ticket', for periods of 9 or 16 days unlimited travel throughout Austria, not just the Alps. The nationwide Rover service is for first or second class travel on Austrian Federal Railway lines, including the Schafberg and Schneeberg Railway lines, as well as the OBB ships on the Wolfgangsee. Most private railways and the Lake Constance shipping companies offer 50 per cent reductions for Rover ticket holders.

Inclusive rail holidays to Austria are available from DER travel, 18 Conduit Street, London W1R 9YD, tel (01) 408 0111.

For genuine railway enthusiasts the Austrian railways **Nostalgic tours** are an excellent way to see genuine old passenger carriages and museum trains restored to mint condition and pulled by old electric locomotives and steam engines. There are 26 different routes to choose from on day outings to various places of interest, with time to explore and sample the local cuisine. Full details are available in the Austrian Tourist office's brochure *Nostalgie-Sonderfahrten*.

A good way to see the Achensee, Tirol's largest lake, is to arrive by the **Achenseebahn**, from Jenbach to Achensee, where Archduke Fedinand II used to entertain his hunting parties with fishing, shooting, hunting and eating. Operational since 1889, this is the oldest still exclusively steam-driven cog railroad of Europe, one of the shortest at 6.7 km (4.1 miles) and one of the steepest, climbing 160 m (525 ft) per km (0.6 mile). It is also one of the narrowest gauge with a one-metre track. The lake terminal at Seespitz is Austria's highest Alpine lake. The 40-minute journey takes the traveller through woodland with fleetingly revealed views to Jenbach, the Inn valley and the Ziller valley to the surrounding Wilder Kaiser massif.

The Zillertal railway travels between Jenbach and Mayrhofen, also powered by steam, with some modern trains, much less popular on the same route. Eighty-five years old, nostalgia is the magnet for modern tourists here, who can play stoker or driver for a few hours and really get a

33. The buffet car.

sharp corners and inclines, all of which keeps the speed down to 25 kph (16 mph). But with such a relaxing way to see Alpine scenery, what is the hurry?

For those interested in flowers, a 15-minute ride on the Reuttener Bergbahn at Lechtal will deposit the traveller at the Alpine flower garden.

TRAINS IN YUGOSLAVIA

The Inter-Rail card is valid in Yugoslavia, but the Eurailpass is not. Yugoslavia is internationally linked to all parts of Europe by train, with new express trains introduced in recent years. In the summer months many seasonal trains are available. Check locally for details. The majority of train services are in non-Alpine regions.

Triglav views by train. From the major town of Ljubljiana, an hour's train ride, by a good regular train service, will take you to the smaller town of Jesenice. From the north, on the Salzburg to Belgrade line, this is the first town after the railway tunnel under the Yugoslav border. From here attractive day walks can be made giving excellent views of Yugoslavia's highest peak, Triglav.

feel for the age of steam. The train runs twice a day during the summer, once a day in winter and is available for charter.

The Stubaital Railroad. From the centre of Innsbruck runs an electric narrow-gauge railway to the entrance to one of Tirol's loveliest valleys, the Stubai. From here the five winter and summer resorts of Schönberg, Mieders, Fulpmes, Telfes and Neustift are in reach, excellent for summer hiking as well as winter skiing, even summer skiing on the Stubai Glacier. The train winds along the Stubai valley across small gorges, viaducts, meadows and woods.

In 1904 this was the first train to be operated on 'monophase alternating current', they will proudly tell you. It set the standard by which the entire Austrian system was electrified a few years later. Along the valley there are eight stops,

CHAPTER NINE

The Alps by Car

. . . Few of the visitors, however, are bent on hard climbing, and the proprietors of carriages and horses apparently fare infinitely better than the guides.
— William Marcet, 1882.

London to Chamonix via Dover is about 650 miles (1050 km). It can be driven in 10–12 hours depending on the number of drivers, the time of day or night, and the route chosen. Easily the quickest French route is by toll autoroutes, which will add some £30 to the cost of the single journey, but considerably cuts the time.

Many other Alpine destinations can be reached in 700 miles (1150 km), though unless you intend to traverse the Alps from end to end, it may well be worth travelling more directly to your destination through Belgium and down the free motorways of Germany for direct access to the eastern Alps.

Increasing numbers of holiday-makers are driving to the Alps, both for winter skiing and summer holidays. Motorways are getting better all the time, as are roads through the Alps. In calm weather the channel crossing can be made in half an hour by hovercraft from Dover to Calais. Boats make the journey in one and a half hours. The Channel tunnel may improve Customs and Immigration hold-ups at each end, but they are usually a formality even now. It is hard to see how a 30-minute journey time can be much improved on, except for those making a direct connection from London to Paris. But with 10–12 hours' driving ahead of you, a few minutes' saving in the tunnel cannot make much difference.

Choice of ferry port will depend on whether you are heading for the western, central or eastern Alps. Dover–Calais is obviously the easiest for the western (French) Alps (Savoie and Dauphiné). For the central and eastern Alps, Dunkerque, Ostend, Vlissingen and Rotterdam may be better routes, since motorway connections start directly. On German motorways high average speeds are possible.

The crossing is only one part of the journey. Other important factors are how quickly you reach the motorways on the other side and the average speed you can maintain on the motorway. In winter cross channel services are less frequent and somewhat cheaper. With bad weather the hovercraft is more likely to be delayed than the boat.

Generally worth looking at are inclusive holidays from many tour operators offering accommodation in the Alps with an inclusive return ferry ticket. They are usually able to obtain substantially reduced ferry rates, particularly attactive if you have a large family or car or both.

1 Mont Blanc,
sunset

2 Powder skiers,
Grindelwald,
Switzerland

3 *Shepherd and his flock above La Grave,*
Dauphiné, France

4 *Spring in*
Switzerland

5 Climber,
Aiguille du Midi,
Chamonix, France

6 Balloon festival,
Chateau D'Oex,
Switzerland

7 *Earth pyramids,*
Ritten, near Bolzano,
Italy

8 *Icefalls and*
crevasses; glacier
on Mont Blanc

9 *Mer de Glace, Monenvers*

10 *Autumn, Dauphiné, France*

11 *Lake Bled,*
Yugoslavia

12 *Drus,*
Mer de Glace,
Chamonix

13 Dawn, Col D'Izouard, France

14 Switzerland by train

15 *Dolomites, Italy*

16 *The Magic Hour,*
Dauphiné, France

DRIVING ON THE SNOW

A few inches (cms) of snow in London, and the capital grinds to a halt. In Scottish ski resorts as soon as there is enough snow to ski, the access roads are blocked. In Europe, however, they are fully equipped to keep the roads free and also to minimize the chances of accidents because of snow and ice on the roads.

In summer in the Alps you can generally expect the roads to be free of snow, but above 2000 m (6500 ft) passes can often have icy and snowy conditions so it is wise for the visiting motorist to arrive in the Alps well prepared at all times of year.

Before travelling to the Alps a good precaution is to contact the AA or the RAC in the UK for up-to-date information on the latest motoring regulations for Alpine countries. They can also help with Green Cards, and special insurance, breakdown and recovery services in

34. *Summer motoring, Lugano.*

Europe. They can also give specific advice for driving in cold weather along the following lines.

The first and most obvious precaution is to check the antifreeze in your car. A stronger solution may be required for the lower temperatures likely to be encountered in the Alps. Check also the hoses and radiator connections since antifreeze has a tendency to find weak spots.

Starting the car in cold weather can be a heavy drain on the battery so if you have a problem do not overstrain the battery, rather try and see if the cold has flattened it. Try the headlights and you will see whether or not it is on full power. It is a good idea to have it checked and charged before leaving home since again the cold will find any weak spots. If a car is left outside in extremely cold winter conditions, the battery will simply not hold its charge. Many ski resorts have heated car parks which are a good investment compared to the inevitable inconvenience and expense of a flat battery. It is a good idea to carry a long set of jump leads. A stopgap is to remove the battery and store it overnight in a warmer place, especially if the car will not be used much while you are staying in the resort.

Another good tip for cold weather is not to use the handbrake. Leave the car in gear when it has stopped. Handbrakes can freeze and jam. In colder Alpine areas, locals often take the precaution of having their engine oil changed to a winter brand which has a lower freezing temperature. Right-hand-drive cars which travel to Europe require a left-hand driving mirror by law as well as a headlamp converter or patch which stops the lights dipping in the wrong direction for Europe.

On the road in bad weather all the basic rules of the road should be followed to the letter. Leave plenty of space in front of you, slow down, avoid heavy or sudden braking. Anticipate manoeuvres well in advance and give clear signals to other motorists. If you do skid, do not touch the brakes. On a rear-wheel-drive car decelerate and steer into the skid.

On snow-covered roads you can travel fast but braking times will be twice or three times the normal. Use lights and wipers in snow storms. Antifreeze should be put into the windscreen washer liquid. Spare blades are useful.

Move off in second gear on the snow and avoid stopping when going uphill; uphill vehicles have right of way. Snow tyres may be a good investment if you are a regular visitor to the Alps in winter. Chains are essential and can be bought here or abroad. Wherever you get them, try them out in a quiet snowless moment. They will be harder to fit in a snowstorm, especially if the flapping instruction sheet is in a foreign language.

In winter, motoring to the Alps is an excellent and fairly cheap way for a group to get to an Alpine ski resort. But the real pleasure of touring the Alps by car is only available in summer when the high passes are open. At any time of year, however, you should study route maps of your proposed journey in advance and make specific enquiries as to the passes, which can be closed suddenly by unexpected snow at any time of year. The Alps have some of the longest cul-de-sacs in the world.

SOME SUGGESTED ITINERARIES

The Napoleon Route – French Alps

'Until I reached Grenoble I was a gentleman adventurer. In Grenoble I became a prince' — Napoleon.

The 'Eagle itinerary' is the route Napoleon took on his return from Elba, from the Golfe Juan to Grenoble and Paris. Follow RN 85 from Grenoble to Golfe Juan, 336 km (208 miles). The Route Napoleon is the tourist name given to the Alpine part of the Emperor's journey from landing at Golfe Juan on 1 March 1815 until his entry to Grenoble on March 7. After Gap and Sisteron it crosses the Bayard pass and enters the Alps proper. It is more common for motorists to drive this route from north to south, since it avoids the crowded 'Autoroute du Soleil' providing a pleasant route from the Alps to the Midi.

Start at Grenoble and travel through Vizille, birthplace of the French revolution; Laffrey, where troops loyal to the Emperor gathered on his return from the island of Elba. The château at Vizille was until 1973 one of the residences of the French president, but now houses the museum of the French revolution. Napoleon's statue can be seen at Laffrey, rallying his troops to the famous 'Prairie de la rencontre' (Field of Meeting). After admiring the landscape at Matheysine and La Mure (see Chapter 8: *The Alps by Train*) one can see Corps where Napoleon spent a night at the Hotel du Palais. The end of the Alpine part of the route is La Sallette where a famous manifestation of the Virgin Mary is believed to have taken place in 1832, and which today is the site of a major pilgrimage. Here one can continue to the Golfe Juan or return to Grenoble.

Swiss Architectural Tour

Well before their modern engineering skills were used to build the Alpine roads and tunnels, spectacular Swiss architecture was perching castles on imposing rock outcrops and cathedrals on city summits. This tour takes in the best.

Starting at Geneva we can see the huge St-Pierre Cathedral in the old quarter, where Calvin preached. Lausanne also has its old town, topped by the gothic Notre Dame, and close by lies the sixteenth-century Sainte-Marie castle, seat of today's cantonal government. On the shores of Lake Geneva is Chillon castle with the backdrop of the Bernese Oberland peaks. At Sion in the Valais, two dramatic buildings catch the eye, the ruined Tourbillon and the Valère with its episcopal relics.

In Ticino, at Locarno the Visconti castle has a

35. Luzern on the Lake of the Four Cantons.

magnificent courtyard. The Lugano cathedral, San Lorenzo, is one of the great achievements of the Italian Renaissance, while at Bellinzona you can see three fortresses dating from the thirteenth to the fifteenth centuries.

In eastern Switzerland the monastery of Disentis-Muster dominates the valley. Saint Gall is famous for its monastic library, while the Gothic and Roman city of Chur has a cathedral with baroque towers. Lucerne, on the Lake of the Four Cantons, beneath Pilatus' peak, is famous for its two covered bridges. Thun castle has antique tapestries while, on the other side of the lake, is the imposing twelfth-century Spiez castle. From Spiez, roads lead up to Adelboden, Kandersteg and Gstaad.

The Dolomite Road – Italy

The road from Bolzano to Cortina was used at the time of the Renaissance by merchants going from Venice to Germany. Modernized from 1895, it was a military road from 1915 to 1918 and for the modern motorist provides wonderful engineering and views such as only the Dolomites can give.

36. The Dolomite road.

Before leaving Bolzano do not miss the chance to travel up to Ritten, by road or cable car from the centre of the city, to see the remarkable earth pyramids at Oberbozen.

Canazei, whence you can reach the Fedaia pass (2057 m/6749 ft), is in the middle of the

84

range, between the Catinaccio, the Vaioletto towers, the Sella massif and the Marmolada, the highest Dolomite peak. It is a common base for walking and climbing in the region.

The Pordoi Pass is the highest and most impressive pass on the Dolomite road, through dramatic gothic scenery between huge rock towers and truncated summits. The western view includes the Sasso Lungo peak. The Siusi Alp (Seiser Alm) is one of the largest summer Alpine pastures, some 40 sq km (15 sq miles) between 1800 m (5900 ft) and 2200 m (7200 ft). Here, at the foot of the Rosengarten group, and the towering Schlern peak, many gentle family walks can be taken. In summer the area is closed to traffic, and makes for pleasant walking.

Another highlight is the Gardena valley, home of the minority group the Ladins, (see Chapter 4: *Alpine People*), who live in lovely surroundings in the main centres of Ortisei, Santa Christina and Selva.

The Marmolada massif is the highest point in the Dolomites and bears their only glacier. A teleferica goes close to the summit with exceptional views. Finally from the Sella pass some of the most extensive Dolomite panoramas can be seen.

An alternative tour is that of the four passes round the Sella massif, the Sella pass, the Pordoi pass, the Campolongo pass and the Gröden pass. Also entertaining for wine enthusiasts in this area is the *South Tirol Wine road*. (See Chapter 10: *Wine and Food of the Alps*.)

The German Alpine Road

The German Alpine road stretches along the southern border of Germany and travels the 1150 km (700 miles) between Lindau on Lake Constance in the west to the Königsee at Berchtesgaden in the east. It is classic German Alpine scenery – peaks mirrored in lakes, and Bavarian villages with their typical onion-shaped church towers. The journey is almost all on high ground, with only the occasional detour into the plains, and will take about three days.

37. Berchtesgaden towers.

Berchtesgaden in the east is covered in Chapter 13: *Skiing in the Alps*, but is also a pleasant place for summer excursions, walking, climbing on the Watzmann and boating to the church of St Bartolomae on the Königsee.

Bad Reichenhall, famous as a spa for the treatment of asthma, has a mountain railway and a Grandhotel which was once a medieval castle.

Ruhpolding is a popular tourist spot in the Chiemgau Alps. Close by is the Gletschergarten, just 15 minutes' walk from the road. This is a museum of glacial erosion.

Reit im Winkel is a summer and winter resort

THE ALPS BY CAR

with views of the Wilder Kaiser and Zahmer Kaiser mountains. It is a good place to see traditional mountain houses topped by bell-towers, roofs weighed down with stones. Wendelstein is famous for its excursion up the mountain railway, see Chapter 8: *The Alps by Train*.

The German Alpine road continues past the Tegernsee (a monastery with beer-brewing monks), Garmisch Partenkirchen (summer and winter resort – see chapter 13), and the Passion play village of Oberammergau. At Fussen, excursions can be made to see some of the most famous royal castles, namely Höhenschwangau and Neuschwanstein. The latter is the best known, open to the public April to September. Its extraordinary fairy-tale appearance is due to the fact that it was designed by a theatrical designer rather than an architect. It is well worth visiting.

The east–west journey winds finally through the Allgau region, one of the great cheese-making regions of Germany, to the Bodensee (Lake Constance) and Lindau.

The Grossglockner scenic route (a route in Hohe Tauern, Austria)

Forty million visitors cannot all be wrong. For this is the number of tourists who have travelled the Grossglockner road through the heart of the Hohe Tauern National park. At the end is the Franz-Josefs-Höhe beside Austria's longest glacier, in front of Austria's highest peak. The drive takes the traveller through meadows, woods, Alpine and mountain landscapes of rocks, snow and ice. Here, once upon a time, Bronze Age huntsmen stalked their quarry; Celts panned for gold; Romans sweated over the Hochtor and mules carried salt and wine; convicted poachers tramped to Venice for enforced naval service. Here in the sixteenth century ten per cent of the world's gold was dug.

The Grossglockner toll road costs 320 AS for a day ticket or 360 AS for a ticket entitling two visits in any calendar year. Many tourists just

drive to the end of the road, gape at the glaciers and the marmots and drive back again. But there are many interesting villages to see on this road where tourism and conservation have found a reasonable balance. A great deal of effort has gone into Alpine museums, sport, and awareness of local heritage.

At Bruch there is a herb instruction path, mountain biking and para-gliding. Fusch has trips in horse-drawn carriages and mountain bike tours. Ferleiten has an animal reserve with brown bears, lynx, wolves and bison. A favourite side trip from here is the night-time ascent of the Edelweiss spitze to see the dawn over the mountains. Heiligenblut is a lovely village with a spectacular Gothic church with golden triptych from Bolzano and a mountaineers' cemetery. Activities include gold washing, riding, and white-water kayaking.

At Grosskircheim there is a gold-mining museum and horse riding along medieval paths from the Hotel Schlosswirt. Winklern has a pilgrimage church and toll tower dating back to AD 1325 when taxes were collected from pack horse drivers.

The Pasterze glacier is 9 km (5 miles) long and covers 20 sq km (7 sq miles). The ice, 250 m (275 yds) thick in places travels at a speed of 50 m (55 yds) per year. From Franz-Josephs-Höhe you can take a railway down to the glacier and walk around on the ice, which is quite safe here for tourists. More strenuous paths are available from this point. In the Alpine hotel at Franz-Josefs-haus, an exhibition details the history of the spot from the time of the visit of the first Emperor in 1856 until the construction of the Glockner road and its operation today. Not surprisingly, restaurants and souvenir shops flourish in this rarefied atmosphere (2369 m/ 7772 ft).

The Austrian Baroque route

This is not a route as such but a selection of 100 masterpieces of the Baroque age of Austria, which is preserved and documented by thou-

sands of buildings and art treasures, many in Alpine regions.

Between 1620 and 1740 Austria's 'heroic age' was crowned by the final banishment of the Turkish threat which had hung over Europe for centuries, or so they see it. During this period Austrian Baroque drew heavily from French, Dutch and Italian influences, blending them into a new and indigenous style in which Austrian was for a time pre-eminent. Ask the Austrian Tourist office for the detailed explanatory route map on Baroque Austria.

Austria from the inside

Another useful if not essential tourist office publication for the motorist in Austria, is the pamphlet *Austria from the inside*. This is an encylopaedic guide to motoring, border cross-

38. The Grossglockner scenic road.

ings, view points accessible by car or train, Alpine passes, toll roads, with distances and suggested itineraries. Circular tours as well as monastery, castle, palace, music and children's itineraries are also covered. In addition there is a detailed country route planning map.

CHAPTER TEN

Alpine Food and Wine

They will dine on mule and mutton made from goats,
They will face the various horrors of Helvetian table d'hôtes;
But where'er the paths that lead them and the food whereon they fare,
They will taste the joy of living as you taste it only there.
— Godley, 1899.

At the turn of the century the Alps – their geography, people and cuisine – were still an acquired taste for the average traveller. Today the food and wines of the Alpine countries are one of the major pleasures of the journey.

In general, Alpine cuisine is the cuisine of people for whom life was hard; the cuisine of short summers, cold winters and limited storage facilities; of an economy which knew how to make the most from the soil. Thus traditional cuisine tended to be very localized, pork from

one valley would be prepared differently from that in the next. We know how wine can taste different from lower to upper slopes, and in the Alps the influence of climate and altitude is even greater.

It is well known that in any international resort cuisine of every denomination may be available, from local to hamburgers to Chinese food. In this summary I have defined Alpine food and wine as that which is produced in Alpine regions and is traditionally Alpine.

FRENCH ALPINE FOOD AND WINE

The best known Savoie cheese is the Tomme, which is best bought in local markets. You should ask to taste it. Look for a nutty flavour, not too chalky nor too smooth. A good Tomme has an attractive crust, grey or speckled with yellow or red. In wine growing areas, grape marc is often added or cumin or fennel. It is a round flat cheese averaging 4 in (10 cm) thick and 8 in (20 cm) round.

Buy Reblochon from farms or markets in the Aravis range. It is a round flat cheese, with a thin yellow, rose or orange crust with a slight white

39. Wines of the Alps: a Dolomite vintage.

dusting. Vacherin is ready at the end of Autumn in the Abondance valley, recognizable by its spruce bark wrapping. It is soft, creamy and mild – eaten with a spoon and delicious with hot boiled potatoes. Abondance comes from the valley of the same name, and tastes between Tomme and Emmental, semi-hard, lots of small holes, sold in rounds 4 in (10 cm) high, weighing 11–13 lb (5–6 kg). Emmental is also made in Haute Savoie. Tamié (a monastic cheese) and Beaumont have a similar taste and are best at the end of the summer.

Beaufort cheese is made in the high pastures of Vanoise, Beaufortin, Tarentaise and Maurienne regions. After six months of preparation the cheeses, which taste slightly of hazel, are ready and weigh about 40 kg (88 lb).

Pork was once practically the only meat eaten in Savoie, and is still widely available. Smoked ham is prepared over large wood fires in the chalets of the Aravis, Upper Chablais and Upper Faucigny regions. Sausages are made in the same way, the most famous being from the village of Magland, near Sallanches. In autumn or winter ask for Les Attriaux or longéoles, large raw sausages flavoured with cumin.

The wines of Haute Savoie are mostly white. Rousette is straw-yellow in colour, with a bouquet varying according to the soil. Drink it chilled as a dessert or aperitif. Ayze wine from near Bonneville is sparkling, dry and fragrant. Crépy, grown on the slopes of Ballaison and Douvaine, and Ripaille, have bottles resembling the wines of Alsace. Marignan is a light and fruity wine and is, like Crépy, good with fish. Buy locally in villages or direct from the vineyards. Apremont and Gentian brandy are also local favourites, producers of much Dutch courage. You can obtain a list of vineyards for visits and tasting from: Syndicat Regional des Vins de Savoie, 3 Rue de Château, 73000 Chambéry, tel 79 33 44 16.

One of the largest liqueur cellars in the world is to be found at Voiron, the Chartreuse distillery, in the massif and near the monastery of the

40. *Vineyard, Dauphiné.*

same name. Other good local products are Chambéry vermouth, cider, and mineral water from Evian on the shores of Lake Geneva.

Alpine food and wine are often combined in the same dish, for example in fondues and Gratin Dauphinois, a simple dish of some gravity made from potatoes, milk, garlic and cream. The Savoie version adds grated Beaufort cheese.

SWISS ALPINE FOOD AND WINE

Swiss wines are not well known in England, mainly because of limited output, but they are good wines nonetheless. In the Valais, Fendant is a dry fruity wine which goes well with any meal, particularly good with cheese. Dôle is a full red wine, which should be served at around 13°C, and is a hybrid of Pinot Noir and Gamay. Johannisberg is a sweet full-bodied wine, best drunk young, good with fish. One of the oldest Valaisian wines is the Humagne, a good 'housekeeping wine' which was once thought to have had curative qualities – a good advertisement.

Good wines of the Lake Geneva area include Perlan, the white Dorin from Vaud and the red

Salvagnin. Neuchâtel has the light and dry Oeil de Perdrix rosé. Swiss beer tends to be pale and weak, but they have some tasty and lethal fruit brandies.

Swiss cheese is one of the country's most famous exports. One third of the total Swiss milk production is turned into cheese, and half of this is exported. Much Swiss cheese is still produced by traditional hand methods to guarantee maturity, originality and purity. Emmental is a versatile cheese for cooking, fondues or eating by itself, with a mild nutty flavour. Gruyère has a strong rich flavour, ideal for sauces, quiches and fondues.

Sbrinz is a hard spicy cheese, good for grating and cooking, or as a tangy appetiser. The Swiss too produce a detailed cheese guide, available from Tourist offices, which informs the visitor of specialist restaurants around the country where cheese dishes can be enjoyed. Tilsit, Vacherin, Royalp, Appenzell and Royalp are just some of the many other varieties the traveller may encounter. Raclette cheese is known for the dish of the same name. To make Raclette the whole cheese is placed in front of the fire, the melted part is sliced off and is served with potatoes or dried meat. You continue melting and slicing until you are full.

Of course the Swiss do not just eat cheese and fondues. Cured dry meats are a great speciality of the mountain regions, especially Bundner-fleisch in the Graubünden region. Look out too for Rösti, fried grated potato, which is eaten at any time of day, with a variety of regional variations. It is mostly found in the German-speaking parts of Switzerland. Indeed in the Region of Château D'Oex, the area where French- and German-speaking Switzerland meet is colloquially known as the 'Rösti line'. One should not of course forget Swiss chocolate, though not strictly an Alpine delicacy. The Swiss eat on average 8 kg (18 lb) of chocolate per annum as compared to the mere 4 kg (9 lb) eaten by the French.

ITALIAN ALPINE FOOD AND WINE

As I have said elsewhere, you can change borders and passports but that does not change the people and their cultures. The South Tirol part of the Alps/Dolomites only became Italian in living memory, so many of its regional speciali-ties are in fact Austrian, Hungarian or distinctly non-pasta in origin. Dishes like Gulash soup will be found in Italy's South Tirol, Austria and most of the Alps, while noodles and strudels are commonplace in South Tirol.

The pasta Alps, mostly the western Italian Alps, have a cuisine which is more recognizably Italian, for example in the Aosta valley where dishes like Aosta valley escalopes, prepared with local veal and cheese, are to be found. Monte Bianco Pudding, a mountainous dessert of chest-nuts and cream is another local speciality. Other

41. The cheese-maker's tools, Switzerland.

42. Market, lake of Lugano.

dishes are less peculiar to the mountains, so that pasta and pizza are common and as good as anywhere in Italy.

Italy is one of the world's largest wine producers. Table wine is cheap and readily available. Like the food, wines of the South Tirol are similar to the wines of the Tirol in Austria.

THE WINE ROAD

Caldaro and Santa Magdalena are enjoyable red wines from this region, while Terlano and Meranese are good too. In the South Tirol, enjoyable excursions can be made along the 'Wine road', through the Überetsch plateau, one of its most picturesque regions. Kalterersee and Gewürztraminer wines come from here and can be widely tasted. At Appiano, 15 million litres (3 million gallons) of wine are produced annually and some 7 million litres (1.5 million gallons) at Caldaro. It is good quality too. At Appiano and all along this wine road you can visit the vineyards and taste freely. At Kaltern/Caldaro you will find the ruins of St Peter Basilica and the South Tirolean wine museum. The best time to

visit here is in springtime or in autumn around harvest-time. Many pleasant walking tours are also possible in the area, which is best explored using Bolzano as a base.

In other Italian Alpine areas, the best Piedmont labels are Barolo, Gattinara and Spanna. In the once French-speaking Aosta, Donnaz and Blanc de Morgex are recommended. As for Lombardy, Valtellina is deservedly popular.

GERMAN ALPINE FOOD AND WINE

The food of the German Alps is the food of Bavaria. An extensive range of sausages (wurst and pork butcher's meats), dumplings known as Knödeln and Spätzle, small meat balls, are common. Lunch tends to be the main meal in Germany. Evening meals are more of a snack – perhaps a speciality dried meat dish. In tourist areas full meals are served in the evenings too.

German wines, which are mostly white, come from the Trier-Würzburg area and between Lake Constance and the Seibengebirge, but you are as likely to be served with a good Austrian wine in the German Alps. Beer is a German speciality, with light, dark and Pilsner beers as well as many local Bavarian varieties.

AUSTRIAN ALPINE FOOD AND WINE

From the Burgenland (until 1920 part of Hungary), comes one of the best known Austrian specialities, the Strudel, and not just the Apfelstrudel. Dough is made from flour and water, with sweet or savoury fillings. Other specialities include cabbage soup, Letscho (smoked bacon stew with tomatoes and red peppers) and paprika, showing the Hungarian influence. Goose is a November favourite. Spicy Liptauer cheese is eaten with dark 'peasant' bread.

'Dumpling Land' is Upper Austria, where the Knödel dough is mixed with sweet or savoury fillings. Smoked meat, Sauerkraut and Semmel-

43. Ski chalet and glühwein.

knödel are also popular in upper Austria. Styrian specialities are 'Sterz', pork with root vegetables and sweet rye bread. Carinthia is also heavily addicted to the noodle, filled with cheese, bacon or ham. The Salzburg equivalent are 'Nockerl'.

Austria is best known for its light table wines or 'offene' open wines, served on draught by the glass. The southern part of Tirol produces good table wines, mostly white, but the country's best wines come from Lower Austria, away from the main Alps, Burgenland and Styria. One of the better red wines is the Tirolean Kalterersee. A white wine favourite is the full-flavoured Gumpoldskirchner. Most whites are better ordered dry. Local beers, e.g. the Zillertaler, regional Schnapps and natural juices (grape and apple juices) are all good.

The organization 'Vinoveritas Austria' produces a detailed brochure on Austrian vineyards and speciality restaurants. Available from Hirtlof 26, A-4283 Bad Zel, tel 072 63/7135, or contact your local tourist office.

YUGOSLAV FOOD AND WINE

In resorts you can eat so-called 'international' cuisine, but in the Alpine regions the food is influenced by Italian and Austrian cuisine too. Yugoslav specialities include *cevapcici, raznjici, and duvec*, forms of pot roasts. There are a number of good red and white wines (Zilavka, Kraski Teran, Postup etc.) as well as the internationally famous Slivovice (plum brandy) which is served as an aperitif.

CHAPTER ELEVEN

Walking in the Alps

'Just put your boots on and go'
— H.W. Tilman

When the last ski lift grinds to a halt, it is easy to think that the Alps are a closed book until the snows of next season begin to fall. But in reality the mountains in summer are an encyclopaedia of new horizons. The passes are mostly open, the snowline recedes and flowers abound. Thousands of kilometres of waymarked trails await the walker.

MAKING A START

Whether you wish to walk or climb, it is wise to have some practice in the UK before arriving in the Alps. The National Mountaineering Centre at Plas y Brenin, Glenmore Lodge and the British Mountaineering Council have excellent introductory courses, or you can contact a mountain guide direct. In European mountaineering centres, many courses are available locally through the *Bureau des Guides* or *Bergführerverein*.

FITNESS

Although good ski legs are a help, fitness is annoyingly specific. The best training for walking is walking. Try and get out in our own hills, even if it is just to wear in your new boots or get used to carrying a back pack.

EQUIPMENT

Good boots will become old friends. Bad boots can be agony. My preference for summer walking is a leather boot with a traditional Vibram sole which is stiff enough to take a crampon, but not so rigid as to be uncomfortable to walk in. Others swear by plastic walking boots with removable inner boots. While these are extremely waterproof from the outside, I find they sweat just as much inside and are less easy to wear into shape. The choice of boot will depend on how much your summer walking will take you above the snowline, whether you intend to return to the valleys at night, stay at a high altitude hut or camp.

Mountaineering clothes are no longer the lacklustre hairshirts they used to be. Designer mountaineering wear is readily available for those who want it. On the other hand it is not essential to spend very much on specialist gear. What you already have in your wardrobe will suffice. Track suits, woollen shirts and sweaters, woolly hat, and ski gloves are all useful.

While it can often be T-shirt-and-shorts weather in the Alps, you still need warm clothing too. A number of layers are better than one thick one for insulation. 'Warm 'n Dry' thermals are a good combination of wool and synthetics which

45. *Walking the dog: Brevent footpath, Drus in background; Chamonix, France* (above).

44. *Paths in the Bavarian Alps* (left).

can cope with a variety of temperatures. One article which is perhaps worth some investment is a good set of waterproofs – I prefer Goretex – which should last some seasons.

A map (1:25,000) and compass are essential, but the rest of the equipment will depend on whether you will be walking above or below the snowline. Above it you will probably need gaiters, crampons, harness, some carabiners, technical climbing hardware, rope and an ice axe. You may not be very clear about how to use the ice axe, but it certainly looks good in your umbrella stand or on the back parcel shelf of your car. You will also need a comfortable pack, with good back support and shoulder straps, and preferably an adjustable waist band to place weight on your hips where it is more easily carried.

Unless you can establish that your chosen route does not involve climbing or travel above the snowline you will need specialist advice on the equipment to take. It goes without saying that if you are not already familiar with the use of ropes and climbing equipment you will need either to go on a course or join a group led by a guide.

WHERE TO GO

Almost anywhere in the Alps can provide interesting walking. Classic areas are the Mont Blanc massif, the Vercors and Mont Aiguille, the Dauphiné Alps (La Grave, La Meije), Berchtesgaden (the Königsee and the Watzmann peaks), Yugoslavia (Lake Bled and Mt Triglav), and the Engadine valley around St Moritz, particularly beautiful in spring and summer.

Chamonix has always been a great favourite with the British in summer, from Edward Whymper to the present day. Dominated by the nondescript bulk of Mont Blanc, the Chamonix valley has a superb selection of walking, bouldering, rock climbing and pure mountaineering, not to mention a plethora of equipment shops where designer mountain wear is *de rigeur*. Easy

footpaths snake up and down the valley, while many pleasant day strolls are accessible by cable car for those who do not wish to waste energy getting off the valley floor. The approach path to the Albert Premier hut gives magnificent but safe views into the gaping jaws of crevasses on the Glacier du Tour.

The Swiss centres of Zermatt and Grindelwald are if anything busier in summer than in winter. Grindelwald and Wengen with the train to Kleine Scheidegg and the Jungfraujoch give access to many fine walks in the 'First' region. From the Jungfraujoch, excursions can be made into the heart of 'glacierland' behind the Eiger. Here too mountain skills and acclimatization are essential.

Accommodation along the way is either in villages (hotels, pensions etc.) camping or staying in a mountain hut. Unless you are able to book a space in advance in a mountain hut it is wise to have a back-up plan in busy periods. While they will not turn you away unless they have to, thoughtless overcrowding can make a hut pretty unpleasant.

The variety of Alpine walks at low and high level is endless. Walks of short duration, even just a couple of hours, can reveal views which would never be afforded to the motorist or train traveller. Others will want to base an entire holiday on walking in a particular area or classic recognized route such as the Tour of Mont Blanc, the Grand Traversée des Alps, the High Level Route from Chamonix to Zermatt (often done on skis), a Via Ferrata (protected by iron ladders and hand rails) or an Alta Via (High Route) in the Aosta Valley or the Dolomites. Here is a selection to start you thinking.

THE TOUR OF MONT BLANC

The Grand Tour of Mont Blanc can be done in 10–14 days. Otherwise known as the TMB, there are a number of variants, none of which should be confused with the Tramway of Mont Blanc (also TMB) mentioned in the chapter on *The*

Alps by Train. The TMB goes right round the mountain, into Switzerland and Italy before returning to France, passing the seven valleys which emanate from the Mont Blanc massif.

Few of the passes on the TMB are above 2400 m (7900 ft), and one would mostly expect them to

46. Grandes Jorasses, Chamonix, France.

be free of snow by July, but walkers should be able to negotiate the odd patch of snow without too much difficulty. Carrying a walker's ice axe would be a wise precaution. It doubles up well as

47. *Walkers approach Mont Blanc.*

a walking stick and a support on tricky ground. August will be even freer of snow, but will have the additional risk of crowds marring the tranquillity of the walk.

Taking the tour clockwise, from the top of the Brévent lift, with some of the best views of Mont Blanc and the Aiguilles de Chamonix, the walker reaches the Aiguilles Rouges, past the Aiguille D'Argentière to the Col des Montets. After crossing into Switzerland over the Col de Balme (2191 m/7188 ft) the TMB drops into the Val D'Arpette, past Champex and up to Val Ferret, abundant in summer flowers. From here good views can be had of Mont Dolent, on whose summit France, Switzerland and Italy meet.

In most villages along the way the walker will find food and accommodation, but camping is possible just about anywhere. Passing the Grand Col Ferret (2537 m/8323 ft) the TMB keeps the Grands Jorasses and the Aiguille de Géant to the right before descending to the French-speaking Italian town of Courmayeur.

The trail climbs again along the Val Veni beneath the terminal moraines of the Brenva face and the Miage. Beyond the Col de la Seigne (2156 m/8254 ft), the Ville des Glaciers lives up to its name, after which, beyond the Col du Bonhomme (2329 m/7641 ft), the Val de Montjoie presents a verdant contrast. Once over the Col de Voza you are once again back in the Chamonix valley and the tour is complete.

Needless to say the walker does not have to set out on the whole of the ten-day trek. Many enjoyable half-day strolls can be had along the 'balcons' of the Chamonix valley, e.g. from Argentière to the cable car at Le Brévent.

THE ALPINE PASS ROUTE

'The Alpine Pass Route', states the introduction to the eponymous book, 'is a little known long-distance footpath which runs along the northern side of the Swiss Alps from the north-east to the south-west of the country.' Jonathan Hurdle has made an attempt – believed to be the first in English – to reveal a high level and yet accessible route through some of Europe's most beautiful high country. The route runs from Sargans in eastern Switzerland to Montreux on the lake of Geneva. The APR was previously an amalgam of existing footpaths, not marked or recognized as a route as such, but loosely described in a now out-of-print tourist office leaflet.

Hurdle's inspiring book describes the route which is suitable for most fit walkers with a couple of weeks summer holiday to spare. The great attraction for many will be that every night of the trip can be spent in the comfort of a Swiss hotel. It sounds like the ideal combination of exercise, mountain splendour and comfort, and the route deserves to become well established. The *Alpine Pass Route* is available from Dark Peak Publishers, Sheffield, England.

THE ALTE VIE (HIGH LEVEL ROADS) OF THE AOSTA VALLEY, ITALY

The Aosta Valley lies south-east of the Mont Blanc Massif, south-west of Monte Rosa. It is easily accessible from the Chamonix valley via the Mont Blanc tunnel. Perhaps best known for the great peaks, Mont Blanc, Monte Rosa, the Matterhorn, the Gran Paradiso, the Aosta valley has Alte Vie (nos. 1 and 2) from Gressoney to Courmayeur and Champorcher.

There are 282 km (175 miles) of paths and mule tracks connecting adjacent valleys, villages and Alpine pastures, being the best way to see local flora and fauna as well as get a feeling for the valley. There are also many side tracks to the Alte Vie as well as ways to link up to valley paths.

Alta Via no. 1 gives the best views of the peaks from Monte Rosa to Mont Blanc, an Italian's-eye-view of the Alps as well as a good look at the traditional rustic dwellings of the Gressoney valley. The Vallone di By in the Ollmont valley, and the Great St Bernard valley are good places to see traditional Alpine life still at work.

Alta Via no. 2 passes largely through the Gran Paradiso National Park. Here there is a good chance to encounter chamois and Ibex and wonder at their seeming ability to jump around the rocks to at least grade five climbing standard, completely without the use of ropes and harnesses. The best time to see flowers is June and July.

The majority of the Alte Vie route is well within the capability of reasonably fit hikers. There are, however, some parts which would cause difficulties for those with little experience of mountain walking. Since the altitude of the Alte Vie varies from 1200 m to 3296 m (4000 ft to 10,800 ft), walkers should expect all types of Alpine terrain, as well as a strong chance of snow lying on the higher sections late into the summer, and sudden changes in the weather.

The best period for these walks is from June to October. During the high season (20 July to 20 September) it is wise to bring a tent, sleeping bag and cooker, since much of the accommodation along the way may be full.

These are just some examples of the type of walks which can be done in the Alps. In fact you can walk just about everywhere in the Alps. In France, Grand Randonnée footpaths are marked on maps and signed on the ground. Almost every Swiss village has informative walking distances and timings marked on neat yellow signs. Many areas have 'Wanderpass' or Reka hiking pass deals with special accommodation rates for walkers. Just ask at the local tourist office and you will be given an area map with routes marked on it. The same applies to every Alpine country.

The great joy about walking is that it is so uncomplicated. Equipment is minimal. Apart from a modicum of conditioning and acclimatization, there is very little that most people have to be told to do. Although anywhere is good for walking, national parks are particularly good venues, because of the lack of intrusion, one hopes, of excessive quantities of the human element.

I can refer the reader to the following detailed guides on walking in the Alps:

Ancient Pathways in the Alps, Caselli and Sugden, George Philip, 1988. This is a fun, modern format walkers book describing in historical, topographic and pictorial detail six classic trade and exploration routes of the Alps. It is well worth putting in your case for planning a walking trip, and historically interesting too.

100 Hikes in the Alps, Spring and Edwards, The Mountaineers, 1979/86. Each hike merits a two-page spread, picture and a few hundred words. This is a useful and informative guide, which gives the length of hike and hours required for each.

Adventuring in the Alps, Reifsnyder, Sierra Club, 1986. Eclectic, country-by-country tour written from an American approach.

Die Schönsten Hohenwegen in Den Alpen, Trenker/Dumler. Sixty of the best high-level walks in the Alps, illustrated in square format – two pictures, a map and detailed text cover each walk. In German.

Les 100 plus belles courses et randonnées du Massif des Écrins, Rebuffat.

Mountain Navigation, Peter Cliff. Written for English hill walkers but the principles are well explained and apply equally to the Alps.

Guide des Refuges et Gîtes des Alpes, Glénat, comprehensive guide to mountain accommodation in the French Alps.

FACTS

Mountaineering courses in the UK:
Plas y Brenin, Capel Curig, Gwynedd, N. Wales, LL24 0ET, tel 06904 214.
Glenmore Lodge, Aviemore, Inverness-shire, Scotland, tel (047) 986 256.

British Mountaineering Council (BMC) courses and mountaineering insurance, Crawford House, Precinct Centre, Booth St East, Manchester M13 9RZ, tel (061) 273 5835.
For a list of British mountain guides write to Plas y Brenin, Glenmore Lodge or the BMC.

In the Alps:
International School of Mountaineering, Club Vagabond, 1854 Leysin, Switzerland, tel (010) 41 (0)25 34 13 21.
Any Alpine mountaineering centre will have an extensive selection of courses. Ask at the local guides bureau.

Organized walking and climbing holidays:
Ramblers, Box 43, Longcroft House, Fretherne Road, Welwyn Garden City, Herts AL8 6PR.
Countrywide Holiday Association, Birch Heys, Cromwell Range, Manchester M14 6HU, tel (061) 225 1000.
Waymark, 295 Lillie Road, London SW6 7LL, tel (01) 385 5015.

Maps: Edward Stanford Ltd, 12–14 Long Acre, London WC2, tel (01) 836 1321.

Equipment: Blacks, 10–12 Holborn, London EC1, tel (01) 404 5681; Snow & Rock, 188 Kensington High Street, London W8, tel (01) 937 0872; Field and Trek, 41 Kings Road, Brentwood, Essex tel 0277 219664.

Alpine Clubs:
USA Alpine Tourist Commission, c/o Chris Zoebeli, Swiss National Tourist Office, Swiss Centre, 605 5th Avenue, New York, NY 10020.
French Club Alpin Française, (C.A.F.) Rue La Boétie 7, Paris 8, tel 47423677.
Swiss Alpine Club Helvetiaplatz 4, 3000 Bern, tel (31) 433611.
Austrian Alpine Club Wilhelm-Greil Strasse 15, Innsbruck, tel 24107.
Italian Via Foscolo 3, Milan, tel 802554.
German Deutscher Alpen Verein (DAV), Prater Insel 5, 8000 Munich 22, tel (089) 235 0900.
Yugoslav Slovene Alpine Association, Dvorzakova 9, Ljubljana, tel 312553.

48. *Below the Mönch.*

'I hope that I shall nowhere be found to have said
"Do as we did", or even "Don't do as we did";
but somewhere or everywhere "Go and do
something".'
— Geoffrey Winthrop Young

CHAPTER TWELVE

Climbing in the Alps

Why is the best blood of England to waste itself in scaling hitherto incredible peaks, in staining the eternal snow, and reaching the unfathomable abyss never to return? . . . Courage is not acquired in a succession of desperate adventures!
— *The Times* (leading article, two weeks after Whymper's success and tragedy on the Matterhorn)

As mentioned in the walking chapter, it is often difficult to draw the line between walking and climbing. Whymper really confused things by entitling his most famous book *Scrambles in the Alps*. Although one might say scrambling is somewhere between walking and climbing, there is little doubt that the exploits for which Whymper was most famous were undoubtedly climbing exploits.

Nor can the test of whether a chosen Alpine adventure is dangerous enough to lead to a fatality be a measure of whether it is climbing or not. A fatal fall could result from a moment of carelessness on an otherwise safe walking path, whereas a competent Alpinist could 'climb' the ordinary route of the Mönch from the Obermönch hut while hardly taking his hands out of his pockets.

The safest approach is simply to see the Alps as mountains; an environment in which many sports are just part of the exploration of the joys and discoveries of mountaineering. Many Alpine walking tours will involve a scramble or two. Most climbs will involve some walking in order to reach the climb.

Prospective Alpinists cannot and should not expect to start from scratch in the Alps. There are many areas of the UK and the USA where pre-Alpine practice can be put in as well as being terrific mountaineering fun in its own right. As with mountain walking, the best practice for climbing is climbing. For all but the most technical and physically demanding climbs, a great deal of the approach will use legs more than arms. These cumulatively exhausting bursts of step climbing soon wear out all but the fittest and most acclimatized. Some major peaks can be climbed in this way, not least Mont Blanc, the Mönch, the Finstraarhorn, and the Aiguille du Tour.

I have selected some of the major Alpine peaks whose ascent has featured greatly in the climbing lore, ancient and modern, of the Alps. Some are feasible to the Alpinist with a couple of seasons' experience, others are only feasible to the most advanced mountaineer, and even then at great risk and more likely with an overnight bivouac. The unifying factor is that they are significant Alpine peaks, not by any means the only significant ones, but ones which have featured in

the history of climbing and Alpine exploration.

For further information on walking and climbing courses, see chapter 11: *Walking in the Alps*, section on Facts.

MONT AIGUILLE

'Mons Inacessibilis', Vercors, France.
Access village Richardière.
Altitude 2086 m (6844 ft).
First ascent Antoine de Ville, 1492.

49. *Mont Aiguille.*

In 1492, the same year when America was being discovered, Antoine de Ville was ordered by Charles VIII to climb Mont Aiguille. This was one of the first recorded ascents in the history of mountaineering. In true military fashion, he engaged stonemasons and carpenters to lay the mountain to siege. With ladders, step cutting, wooden supports which were little short of mountain scaffolding, they reached the summit in late June. So much for the arguments as to aided climbing which were to besiege the post-war climbing years. Antoine de Ville stayed six days on the summit. He built a shelter and said Masses, presumably for his safe return. He was obviously not in a hurry to repeat the experience, which he later described as 'one of the most horrible and terrifying passages I have ever seen'. The mountain was not to be climbed again until 342 years later, by a local shepherd who was quite unaware of his second place in the history of the mountain.

At the time the ascent of Mont Aiguille was one of the most startling events of the era, comparable with the first moon landing of the modern age. It certainly attracted easily as much waffle in contemporary and later press, de Ville being accused of using alchemy and magic to gain the summit. Rabelais, in full flow in his *Quart Livre de Pantagruel*, described Mont Aiguille as 'the sheer unsteady peak, shaped like a pumpkin . . . [on which] . . . the king's conductor . . . with wondrous machines, climbed to the very top'. The machines were no more than the standard military castle-storming gear of the time.

Today the surrounding area is a regional park, with rustic hamlets and villages at Chichiliane and St Michel les Portes, where locals live off the land. Some even still share a common oven. Dramatic views of this almost Dolomitic peak can be had from all sides, in particular from above St Michel les Portes, just off RN75.

MONT BLANC

Access village Chamonix, France.
Altitude 4807 m (15,771 ft).
First ascent Paccard and Balmat, 1786.
Time required for 'normal' route 2–3 days via the Goûter or Grand Mulets route.

'The Mont Blanc which, like the God of the stoics, was a great beast whose frozen blood circulated eternally within its veins of stone.' — Shelley.

On a busy summer day, the 11,000 residents of the Chamonix valley may entertain tens of thousands of tourists, while 300 climbers will attempt the summit of Mont Blanc. The idea of climbing to the summit of Mont Blanc was first hatched by the Genevese Horace Benedict de Saussure, who offered a prize for the first to the summit. Paccard and Balmat reached the summit on 7 August, 1786. Balmat, a glass cutter and crystal hunter, had made a previous reconnaissance in June of the same year, being one of the first to spend a night out on the mountain (near the Bosses ridge) and return to tell the tale.

History and rumour suggest Balmat was the real mountaineer of the two, while his partner Paccard, a doctor, was branded the amateur, less interested in the reward, more in glory. His part in the achievement was not helped by the fact that during the ascent he lost his hat and quickly went snowblind. They made a victorious return to Chamonix holding hands, not out of friendship, rather from necessity.

The Mont Blanc massif has some 400 summits, 71 glaciers, as well as an off-piste ski run, the Vallée Blanche, 16 km (10 miles) long. Today a 'normal route' ascent is done in two or three days. The Goûter route is approached by the Mont Blanc Tramway to Nid D'Aigle, thence to the Goûter refuge at 3817 m (12,523 ft). From there, climbers leave the hut at 0100 or 0200, climbing over the hard snow to the Vallot Refuge (4362 m/14,311 ft), reaching the summit at (4807 m/15,771 ft) by perhaps 0800 or 0900. A number of descent routes should put the party back in Chamonix the same day. An alternative is via the Aiguille du Midi cable car to the Grands Mulets refuge, by a steeper climb to the Vallot refuge and by the same route along the Bossons ridge to the summit.

Mont Blanc by these 'ordinary routes' is not considered a technically difficult mountain, particularly late in the season when, with luck, the ascent to the Goûter hut will be fairly clear of snow. However, it is one of those mountains which breeds its own weather. Winds high enough to defeat a summit bid may reach 60–100 mph (100–160 kph) at any time on the ridges while all in the valley is sunny and still. Just as frequently bad weather or lack of acclimatization forces parties to turn back. From a weather viewpoint, one in three attempts are successful. On that reckoning I should make it next time.

Both the Goûter and Grand Mulets refuges have guardians and provide food and blankets but become busy and should be booked in advance by ringing the Club Alpin Français. The Vallot refuge is not somewhere you would want to book in advance. It is a tin shack with no facilities, knee-high with detritus, whose only benefit is as a waymark and shelter from the wind.

While the normal routes take two or three days, Europe's highest mountain attracts record breakers. In 1864 the Briton Morshead made the return trip from Chamonix to the summit in 16 hours, a Frenchman Louis Bailly-Bazin in 8 hours 10 minutes in 1975, and 1986 two Savoyards Cusin and Gazan in 7 hours 56 minutes.

LES DRUS

Access village and its altitude Chamonix, France.
Altitude 3745 m (12,316 ft).
First ascent Clinton Dent, 1876.

The Drus is a unique mountain, coupled with the Aiguille Verte (4121 m/13,520 ft) in the heart of the Mont Blanc massif. Many great mountaineering achievements are closely linked to its name. In the 1940s Pierre Alain climbed the north face for the first time. The west face, once considered unconquerable, was finally opened by a French team. The Americans opened a new direct route on the west face, making a further climbing landmark, the 'American Direct'. Some years later Walter Bonatti took nine days to solo the south-west pillar which now bears his name.

The Drus also attracts some of the more

50. *Drus and Aiguilles Vertes.*

unusual elements in mountaineering. One summer morning in 1988 at 0745, stuntman and snow surfer Bruno Gouvy boarded a helicopter which took off from the Chamonix valley. Had he forgotten his lift pass and his skis? Had he taken leave of his senses? Not exactly – he had something rather unusual in mind for today's entertainment. Fifteen minutes later he made a last check on his parachute harness and freefall jumped 1500 m (5000 ft) above the summit of the Drus.

Only when he was 500 m (1600 ft) above the summit did he pull the rip-cord, opened his parachute and skilfully guided it to a pinpoint landing on a 15 sq m (18 sq yd) platform. If he missed, there was 1000 m (3300 ft) of void on every side.

Having made a successful landing he continued his unique descent to the valley, abseiling

500 m (1600 ft) down the notorious north face of the Drus until he reached the Drus Niche. The Drus Niche is one of the most difficult snow slopes of the Alps. It is a gigantic snow-covered slope suspended in the middle of a vertical rock face. The angle varies from 50 to 55 degrees, compared to the 30 or 35 degrees of an average pisted black run. Bruno had decided to snow surf down it, having estimated that it would take about an hour.

Finally, at about noon, Bruno finished his morning's frolic by clipping himself into his hang-glider to fly 700 m (2300 ft) down to the base of the mountain, being back in the valley in time for lunch! A remarkable peak and a remarkable feat.

LA MEIJE

Access village La Grave, Dauphiné, France.
Altitude 3983 m (13,067 ft).
First ascent Boileau de Castelnau, with the two Gaspard guides, 16 August 1877.

In 1870 Coolidge and his aunt reached the Pic Central of La Meije, only to find later that not this but the Grand Pic, to which they could find no route, was the highest peak on the Meije. However, it was a remarkable ascent in itself, not least because their dog Tschingel established a canine altitude record for the Alps. While the occasional dog is still seen at surprisingly high altitudes even today, they are better confined to the Surrey hills.

Despite Coolidge's aunt's hope that the Meije would 'save herself for me' Boileau de Castelnau beat her to the summit, after 17 attempts, in 1877. It was one of the last major Alpine peaks to keep its head, when all around were losing theirs. The access town of La Grave may be less well known to tourists, but to climbers it is as famous as Chamonix or Zermatt. While well equipped with hotels and facilities it has none of the affluence of these other centres being a modest but dramatically situated Dauphiné village.

For non-climbers the Téléférique des Glaciers de la Meije goes to 3200 m (10,500 ft) and offers superb views of the hanging glaciers and sheer faces of La Meije. The mountain, which a century ago had no more than a handful of routes to its summits now counts over a hundred in the Groupe de Haute Montagne's guidebook.

THE MATTERHORN

Access village Zermatt, Switzerland.
Altitude 4476 m (14,691 ft).
First ascent Whymper, 1865.
Time required for 'normal' route One to two days via the Hörnli hut.

The Matterhorn was still unclimbed in 1861 on the arrival of Whymper in Zermatt. Zermatt guides were of the opinion that it was unclimbable, but from the Italian side it appeared that the route might be easier. The Italian guide Carrel had reached 3800 m (12,467 ft) in 1859. Whymper made a number of unsuccessful attempts in the next few years.

In 1865, Whymper tried to hire Carrel, the leading guide at the time, but Carrel was strangely elusive about his commitments until it became clear that he too had his eyes on the summit. Returning to Zermatt, Whymper hastily put together a party of mixed ability and the race was on.

They reached the summit ahead of the Italians, led by Carrel from the other side, and spent 'one crowded hour of glorious life' on the summit. Seeing the Italians coming up the other side, they showered them with stones, to make sure there was no misunderstanding about who was the first to the summit.

Their objective achieved, they began the descent. It is thought that Hadow, one of the least experienced party members, slipped, causing guide Croz to lose balance and fall. The others, who were roped together, lost their footing and fell as one. What then happened is unclear. In any event they seem to have been poorly belayed, but the rope broke (some have

suggested it was cut) and four fell to their deaths. Three bodies were later recovered, but one is still out there. This was a horror story which captured the imagination of the European press and put the rationale behind climbing very much in dispute.

But the sport continued. Today there are refuges on the Italian side (Rifugio Carrel) and the Swiss side (Hörnli hut) which enable the climber to attempt the mountain in one or two days. Fixed ropes are everywhere, and some guides have been known to take two sets of clients up in a single day. But even the 'ordinary route' is a serious undertaking at any time of year because of altitude and weather.

THE EIGER

Access village Grindelwald and Wengen, Bernese Oberland, Switzerland
Altitude 3975 m (13,041 ft).

51. The Matterhorn seen from the summit of the Finstraarhorn.

First ascent Charles Barrington (1858); north face – Heinrich Harrer's party (1938).

The ordinary route on the Eiger is not unusually difficult by Alpine standards. It is not especially high or technically challenging. It was first scaled by the amateur jockey Charles Barrington on his first visit to Switzerland. Unimpressed by the Jungfrau, and blissfully unaware of the reputation the north face was later to gain, he dragged his guides up and down it in a day.

But it was the north face which forged the Eiger's reputation as a killer mountain. After the north faces of the Matterhorn and the Grandes Jorasses had been climbed, the north face of the Eiger became 'the last great problem of the Alps'. It rises some 1800 m (5900 ft) sheer from the screes. As recently as 1858 the north wall was described as 'an area of objective danger which by all the laws of mountaineering should remain untouched'. It is probably these very sentiments which have made it such a magnet for mountaineers as well as the author of so many fatalities. After the Mont Aiguille, Mont Blanc and the Matterhorn, the Eiger has inspired more voyeurism and press interest than any other Alpine peak in its time.

The first attempt on the north wall in summer ended in rescue from the Eigerwand window in the railway station. Then in 1935 came death, frozen to the rock, for two Munich climbers. The objective dangers of rock fall are perhaps the worst, since however experienced the mountaineers this is a totally unpredictable danger. Winter was later realized to be in some ways easier, since the process of disintegration of the rock face is halted by the big chill.

In 1937 a German and Austrian party came to grief in a much-publicized rescue watched by the world's press from Kleine Scheidegg. The Swiss promptly banned attempts on the north wall, which did nothing except whip up further interest. Still parties tried and failed.

The President of the Alpine Club in England considered the Eigerwand to be an obsession for the 'mentally deranged . . . the most imbecile variant since mountaineering began'. But still they came, gravity-defying but not death-defying lemmings. In 1938 Heckmair and Vorg teamed up with the two Germans Harrer and Kasparek to make the first successful attempt on the North Wall, receiving commendations from Hitler for their pains. Harrer was later to write the gripping history of the Eiger in *The White Spider*.

After the intervention of the war the suicidal slaughter went on. Desperate rescue attempts in hanging baskets from the summit, death after six or seven days' exposure on the face, bodies found two years after their deaths only an hour from safety – these were almost commonplace events.

The first winter ascent was made in 1961, the first solo in 1963. In 1966 an Anglo-American team put up the first direct route up the middle of the face, but not without the death of John Harlin, the American who had conceived the idea of the direct line, who fell from fixed ropes.

THE PELMO

Access Cortina D'Ampezzo, Italian Dolomites.
Altitude 3168 m (10,393 ft).
First Ascent John Ball, 1857.

The Pelmo was one of the first great Dolomite peaks to be climbed. It can be approached from the main Ampezzo valley road and is well seen towering above San Vito, the Faleria path, or, from the other side on the road between Caprile and Selva di Cadore up the Val Fiorentina.

John Ball made his attempt on the summit in September 1857, with a local chamois hunter. Not for the first time in the history of climbing, they reached a spot where an Alpine hunter was unnerved and began to put imagined difficulties in the way of the ascent. But Ball would not be dissuaded. He calmly rearranged the crumbling rock and, despite the entreaties of his guide, they gained the summit ridge in passing 'from one jagged and rotten tooth to another.' Ball summarized his thoughts on the Pelmo: 'a gigantic fortress of the most massive architecture, not fretted into minarets and pinnacles, like most of its rivals, but merely defended by huge bastioned earthworks, whose walls in many places fall in sheer precipices more than 2,000 feet (700 m)'.

Although his nerves had been tested, they certainly had not failed him. Today the area is still comparatively unknown and unspoiled, despite the road access to the attractive Val Fiorentina and the Valle di Zoldo.

THE GROSSGLOCKNER

Access village Heiligenblut and Franz-Josef-Höhe (2418 m/7933 ft) via the Grossglockner Strasse, Hohe Tauern, Austria.

Altitude 3797 m (12,457 ft).
First ascent organized by the local bishop, 1800.

The Grossglockner is Austria's highest mountain. Heiligenblut on the way up has one of the main mountaineering schools in Austria, which transfers to Franz-Josefs-Höhe in summer months at the end of the Grossglockner highway. The 10 km (6 miles) Pasterze Glacier (third longest in the Alps) can be seen just below the car park, along with a colony of scrounging marmots who have substituted for their natural diet a far more reliable bounty of crisps, sandwiches and chocolate from the ever-present colony of tourists.

The 'ordinary' route up the Grossglockner starts from the edge of the glacier (the Hoffman's Hut – one hour on a level path from the car park) to the Adlersruhe (3466 m/11,371 ft). It is not a technically difficult peak, but quite arduous.

TRIGLAV

Access village Kranjska Gora, Mojstrana, Trenta, Julian Alps, Yugoslavia.
Altitude 2864 m (9396 ft).
First ascent by the German doctor Willonitzer, with three local guides, 1778.

Towering above its neighbours, Triglav's summit view is, not surprisingly, extensive with the Aljaz tower and the Triglav glacier on the north face, the only Yugoslav glacier. The challenging north face is an impressive 1250 m (4000 ft) high. The summit is frequently in cloud. The brooding malevolence of the north face is accentuated by the sharp echoes of rock fall in a dramatic arena. Standing in front of the face, it is easy to believe this mountain has a spirit. Approaching from other directions, there are numerous footpaths to the summit which would be suitable for walks for one or two days, with convenient huts.

One such hut is the Kredarica hostel, largest in the Julian Alps. The western approach to Triglav is the Trenta valley and the hamlet of Na Logu, with the Zlatorog mountain hut, the Planinski Orel hostel, a mountain museum, camping and rooms to let. Nearby is a mountain guides' and military cemetery. The road leads as far as the Aljazev Dom, from where a 15-minute walk takes the traveller right under the north face, by the monster piton memorial to wartime Yugoslav mountain partisans.

There is a mountain garden at the Juliana Alpinetum, which boasts of over 900 species of mountain flowers in spring and summer.

The pioneer of the Julian Alps, Julius Kugy, is remembered in a monument by the side of the Vrsic road, near Na Logu. His *Five Hundred Years of Triglav* traces its history since 1452, while his *Alpine Pilgrimage* is his mountain memoir.

'If climbers remained as good and pure in the plains as they were in their ideal moments on the summit, other men, seeing them return, would believe them to be a troop of angels descended from heaven. But climbers when they go home, become once more prey to their weaknesses, resume their bad habits, and write their articles for Alpine journals . . .'

— Guido Rey, *Peaks and Precipices: Scrambles in the Dolomites and Savoy*, 1914.

52. *The malevolent north face of Triglav,*
    Yugoslavia.

CHAPTER THIRTEEN

Skiing in the Alps

This is not appreciated yet, but I am convinced that the time will come when hundreds of Englishmen will come to Switzerland for the skiing season.
— From 'An Alpine Pass on Ski', by Sir Arthur Conan Doyle, 1894, *Strand Magazine*: one of the first commissioned pieces of ski journalism. How right he was!

THE HISTORY OF ALPINE SKIING

Unlike skiing in Scandinavia, where its history dates back 3000 years and has always been part of folklore and daily winter life, skiing in the Alps is barely a century old.

We have already seen how, since the 1800s, the English started to visit the Alps in summer and winter, principally to walk and climb. But in the early days winter sports were confined to skating, tobogganing and mountaineering. The chief British pioneer of recreational skiing was Sir Arnold Lunn at the turn of the century, who developed an 'Alpine' style of skiing. Another Briton, Vivian Caulfield, was an adherent of the Norwegian style of skiing. A third main pioneer was the Austrian Zdarsky, who made extensive research on bindings and the then complicated process which we now call turning. In the early days a stout stick was used to slow progress, and if this did not work the skier just threw himself onto the snow.

Wengen and Mürren in Switzerland were the first to entertain ski tourists, from whom most of the day would be occupied in climbing uphill in order to ski down – there were no lifts. The first recorded ski race was held in 1903 in Davos, followed by slalom races with gates. Races were mostly organized by private clubs such as the Public Schools Alpine sports club, and the Kandahar. The members generally were well off, since it was a long time before skiing was to become a sport for the masses. The British National Championship in Wengen in 1921 and the 1929 Arlberg Kandahar recognized Downhill for international competition rather than the Scandinavian disciplines of langlauf (cross country) and ski jumping.

In 1924 the Federation International de Ski (FIS) was formed and the first Winter Olympics were held in Chamonix. Alpine skiing as a recognized sport was finally established by the Third Winter Olympics in Garmisch Partenkirchen in 1936.

TECHNIQUE

Technique has been the main revolution in the last 50 years of skiing. Early turns were made by

telemark (a Norwegian turn) or by the stem Christie. The parallel Christie was developed in the 1930s, and became the basis for modern skiing. By the 1960s this had further been refined by Jean-Claude Killy, whose 'banking' technique swept the board in many international races as well as achieving three gold medals in the 1968 Winter Olympics. As in motoring, many racing techniques filter back to the general public in skiing and fall into common use.

The 1960s saw a great increase in world travel and skiing was no exception. Some Alpine villages carefully extended their existing chalets to accommodate the demand, whereas others constructed tower blocks such as at La Plagne which were efficient but downright ugly. Ski lift technology came on apace. In 1945 Austria had 12 cable railways, in 1987 there were 4000 lifts.

Wartime need produced new metals technology and much of this was used in ski production, which moved on from the metal-edged wooden ski of yore.

Aluminium was overtaken by fibreglass and sophisticated lamination techniques, encouraged by racing successes. After the 1970s the accepted ski length was shortened from arms length above your head to perhaps six in (15 cm) above. Useful learning techniques such as 'ski évolutif' made learning easier, with skis short to begin with, becoming longer as the skier progressed. As skis become more sophisticated and easier to turn, length is on the increase again. Boot technology has moved on too, from leather to space-age materials.

EQUIPMENT

Equipment can be a headache for beginners and intermediate skiers. Beginners will quickly grow out of their first skis and boots so it is unwise to buy at first instance – rent until you gain an idea

53. Berchtesgaden.

of what suits you best. Unless they fit perfectly, hired boots can be very uncomfortable. Buy your first boots when you reach intermediate standard. When buying skis, many shops have a useful 'try before you buy scheme'. Make sure your skis and bindings are serviced before each holiday, and don't forget to take out winter sports insurance. Good sunglasses and strong suncream are important even on hazy days.

CROSS COUNTRY SKIING

Downhill skiing is not the only skiing which can be done in the Alps. Cross country skiing has a wide following in all the Alpine countries, under the name 'Ski de Fond' (France) and 'Langlauf' (Switzerland and Austria). Burning up more calories than almost any other sport, cross country can vary from an easy day out with the family to a marathon race. Equipment is cheap, there are no lift passes to be paid for, and it is easier to make a start at cross country than downhill skiing with all the problems which altitude and gravity imply.

Most Alpine valleys which have regular winter snow cover have kilometres of prepared cross country trails with loops (loipes) and A to B routes. Look for the 'Foyer de ski de fond' in French-speaking parts and the 'Langlaufzentrum' in German speaking resorts. This is where the tracks begin, where equipment can be hired and lessons arranged.

The Worldloppet is the international series of races for cross country ski racing and organizes a number of international ski marathons. In the Alps you can watch or even take part in:

The Dolomiten Lauf – based in the city of Lienz in Austria, with some 3500 skiers who ski for 60 km (37 miles).

The König Ludwig Lauf – the longest of the Worldloppet events over 90 km (56 miles), starting at Ettal, passing Oberammergau and mad king Ludwig's nineteenth-century castle. Also about 3000 skiers.

The Engadin ski marathon – in the St Moritz

area of Switzerland, the world's largest cross country race with over 12,000 competitors, along the classic marathon distance of 42 km (26 miles), one of the flattest races.

The Marcialonga – the Italian Dolomite event with some 5000 skiers, from Moena to Cavalese, through the Fiemme and Fassa valleys, 70 km (44 miles).

SKI MOUNTAINEERING

Ski mountaineering is a developing sport among the British and certainly very popular with Alpine countries. Using special skis and bindings, skiers are able to travel uphill as well as downhill, thus obviating the need for ski lifts. In the high mountains tours off the beaten track across virgin snow, glaciers, and inaccessible cols can be made quite out of sight of ski resorts and away from the madding crowd.

Tours can be made just for a day, or a week. Skiers stay overnight either in mountain huts or descend to the level of ski resorts. Such tours depend on a special lifting heel binding and artificial seal skins which grip on the snow for uphill traction. Other equipment is carried in a back pack. The ski mountaineering season is from February to May, often at high altitude. It requires stamina, skill and a strong skiing standard, usually in the company of an experienced mountain guide. It is hard work but highly rewarding.

Many areas of the Alps are suitable for ski tours, one of the most famous of which is called the Haute Route, or High Level Route, from Chamonix to Zermatt, taking 7–10 days. In recent years this has become over-popular, but the Alps are full of equally interesting and suitable ski mountaineering areas.

54. Cross country skiers in Germany.

THE NEW WAVE

Just when we thought we had run out of possibilities for new ski design, along came the new wave – mono-skiing and snow surfing. The principles of mono-skiing have very little to do with mainline piste skiing, except that you do need to use a lift to get to the top and this is where the problems start. You may cut quite a dash in the lift queue, but actually travelling up a ski-tow may be infuriatingly difficult. Once out on the snow, the sensations are unique, styles vary and some would say that mono and surf are the ultimate in free expression on the snow. Both are more fun in soft off-piste powder. Les Arcs in France has become established as a centre for learning the new wave snow sports, but many resorts can hire out the boards and provide instruction.

THE WORLD CUP CIRCUIT

The World Cup ski-racing circuit spans Japan, the Americas, even Australia, with many events in the Alps. Traditional start is the 'Première neige' at Val D'Isère in France. Locations change slightly from year to year for the main disciplines of Downhill, Slalom, Giant Slalom, Super Giant Slalom and Combined. Competitors can enter for the overall World Cup or specialize in individual events.

In *France* the main World Cup locations are Val D'Isère, Val Thorens, Les Menuires, Chamonix and Morzine. *Italy* has Sestrière, Courmayeur, Madonna de Campiglio, Val Gardena and Val Zoldana. *Switzerland*'s venues are Crans Montana, Adelboden, Wengen, Grindelwald. *Germany* has Oberstaufen, Pfronten, Garmisch Partenkirchen. *Austria* – Mellau, St Anton, Kitzbühel and Altenmarkt. *Yugoslavia* has Kranjska Gora and Maribor.

SKIING IN THE AUSTRIAN ALPS

Second only to skiing, you might say that the Austrian national sport is 'Gemütlichkeit' (being

nice to people). If you have been there before, it is always wonderful to be back. If it is your first time you will be made equally welcome. Austria is a world away from the impersonality of purpose-built ski people factories. There is a totally different concept of skiing accommodation to France and Switzerland.

Although in all Alpine countries you will find hotels of different categories, there are very few self-catering apartments in Austria. When skiing on a budget in Austria you book bed and breakfast in a private village Gasthaus. The accommodation is traditionally furnished and invariably spotless. Most houses have up-to-date facilities. Some have rooms with washbasin, others have private bathrooms.

Since so many skiers book bed and breakfast in this way, everyone eats out in village restaurants, which tend to be plentiful and comfortably busy. Table space is at a premium and is frequently shared. This quickly breaks the ice with strangers and creates an instant social life. The ice-breaking process is greatly assisted by Austrian 'designer glühwein' which some still think is the best in the Alps. Cheaper resorts are still available, but tend to be at low altitude. Like most places, in Austria you get what you pay for. Good resorts with a good snow record cost money.

Kitzbühel is an international resort in an ideal location at the hub of its own ski circus. The home of the famous Hahnenkamm downhill race lies in a snow pocket which holds good snow from December to March. Ski safaris, powder skiing, and ski touring are available in addition to a large area of easy pistes. Road, rail and air access are all excellent. Good *après ski* enhances this picturesque thirteenth-century Tirolean walled town.

55. Slalomer, Wengen.

Zürs is one of the few purpose built Austrian resorts, and still retains a lot of traditional charm. It has a long snow-sure season, with hotels which tend to be expensive but are still good value. The resort is linked with Lech and St Anton on the Arlberg ski pass, probably the best skiing in Austria.

St Anton is traditionally Tirolean, but international, perhaps too much so. Despite its medium altitude it has fantastic skiing and is part of the Arlberg ski pass, linked to Lech and Zürs. St Anton is a resort which you can hate or love. One of the top Austrian resorts, it attracts skiers of all standards, but is particularly suited to good skiers. New lifts and snow cannons have improved facilities. Its ski school, with more than 300 instructors, is world famous. Focal point of the resort is the main street, much improved since being pedestrianized.

The sports centre offers skating, indoor tennis, squash and indoor swimming. Locals are friendly and English is widely spoken. Social life very Austrian — sleigh rides, knee slapping, yodelling, zither music, tea dancing at the Krazy Kangaruh or sophisticated Hotel Post, as well as dustbin-liner descents of the nursery slopes.

On the down side, the success of ski school means some classes are a bit too large. Some walking in the village is required to and from connecting lifts. Despite new lifts, some queuing persists.

SKIING IN THE SWISS ALPS

This is the land of efficiency, chocolates and lace. Set your watch by the clockwork trains and clockwork cuckoos. This renowned Swiss efficiency is reflected in the Swiss hotel service, which is arguably the best in the world. Every detail of your stay in a Swiss hotel is carefully attended to, even to turning down your duvet at night.

Most Swiss ski resorts are at a good altitude, in contrast to many smaller Austrian resorts.

Public transport by rail and bus is excellent, which makes midweek transfers easy. But taxis are an expensive luxury.

Switzerland's other great reputation with the British is that it is expensive, but this is not necessarily so. Certainly you do get good value for your money in hotels. They may actually be cheaper than France and better value, star for star, then their neighbours.

Swiss standards in all departments of the holiday experience are probably the highest in the Alps, with the possible exception of cuisine. The food, while always being of the best quality, can be bland as well as deserving that most pejorative of terms, 'international'.

Lift systems are not so well connected as France, and you will probably do a bit more walking in Switzerland. However, most resorts now include a free skibus in the price of the skipass.

Atmospherically, Swiss resorts are perhaps the best in the Alps. Architecture is attractive. Nightlife is good, because tourism is based on hotels, not apartments. Half-board in hotels is cheaper than taking bed and breakfast pension and eating out.

Being in a country whose resorts are based on hotels, self-catering apartments are not particularly cheap. The Swiss cannot persuade themselves to assume the French habit of sardining hordes of people into tiny apartments. But this is all part of the quality Swiss deal. A Swiss four-person apartment genuinely accommodates four people, whereas the French might jam eight into the same place. But perhaps if the Swiss did jam eight into a four-person apartment they might see the funny side of life a little more often than they do!

Flims-Laax is a composite resort in a sunny valley linked by a common ski pass. The extensive 'white arena' has runs for all standards. You will enjoy the stunning scenery and benefit from the well-equipped lift systems. Attractive chalets and hotels radiate from the main square, which is dominated by the tall pine trees so characteristic of the area.

Verbier is one of the world's great resorts, whatever your skiing standard. Accommodation is mostly in traditional chalets. There are limitless off-piste skiing opportunities, and challenging black mogulled pistes. Nursery slopes are extensive, with kindergarten for ages three to ten. If it sometimes gets very busy, the great skiing is compensation enough.

St Moritz is where even the ski bums drive BMW's . . . Fur coats, private jets, private ski instructors, the Cresta run, ski 'poseurs' and good skiers too. Cross country, the Engadine valley . . . a superlative resort. Sophisticated and fashionable, St Moritz has plenty to amuse both the skier and the après skier. But the Engadine valley is not just St Moritz. It has much more to offer in terms of small charming Romansch villages which give access to the Engadine at non-jetset prices.

The Engadine valley

Celerina is a picturesque old hamlet at the bottom of the Cresta run, with village atmosphere and prices, yet connected directly by cablecar with the St Moritz skiing at Corviglia. **Pontresina** is a quiet resort of considerable charm a couple of miles from St Moritz and closer to some of the best Engadine skiing at Diavolezza and Lagalp. **Silvaplana** is a charming lakeside village with picturesque church, at the foot of the Julierpass. **Champfer** is a tiny resort between the Silvaplana and St Moritz lakes, complete with gothic church. **Sils Maria and Surlej** are charming villages. In **St Moritz** itself, **Dorf** is the magnet for the rich, while **St Moritz-Bad** is the downmarket part of town, still pleasant by most standards.

High altitude usually guarantees good snow cover. Skiing is excellent at all standards, though you must be prepared to travel around the valley to get the most out of it. Apart from the many obvious facilities available in St Moritz (shops, *après ski* etc.), a great deal of the attraction is watching and rubbing shoulders with the rich and famous in the resort every other resort likes to copy.

The area can be expensive if you do not shop around. Transfers from Zürich airport are not quick, but considerably enhanced by the Glacier Express train from Chur. Nursery slopes are not always very convenient. Lift queues can be bad in high season. Ground space in St Moritz is so expensive that you get skyscrapers crammed together in St Moritz Dorf. Views can be disappointing and ugly, when you should be seeing undiluted mountain splendour.

SKIING IN THE FRENCH ALPS

France is probably best known to the British for high density apartments and purpose-built motorway resorts, where lift systems are often excellent, well connected, and reduce queues to a minimum. Also, if you are on a budget, the well-filled apartments (where a bed has been squeezed in every nook and cranny) can be real money savers, especially with self-drive.

But many have obviously had their fill of soulless highrise blocks and crave after a genuine Alpine village with good facilities. These do exist in the shape of Megève and la Clusaz among others. These are both traditional resorts with an indigenous local population rather than a work-force imported for the winter. The fact that the hotels tend to be family-run distinctly improves the atmosphere. There are a few villages recently constructed in Savoyard style which combine Alpine charm with the convenience of a modern ski resort – hotels and apartments right on the piste with plenty of lifts to get out of the valley, e.g. Valmorel, Belle Plagne, Lauze 1800 and Vaujany (Alp D'Huez).

Ski évolutif – skiing without tears

One of the great non-culinary creations to emerge from France in recent years, ski évolutif is an ideal way for the late starter or non-athlete to start skiing. In a number of modern resorts like Les Arcs, Flaine, La Plagne and Valmorel, results are rapid and gratifying.

Starting on skis about one metre long, learners then ski on 135 cm and 160 cm skis before going on to normal length. The shorter skis enable you to gain confidence quickly and get through those often dreadful first few days when all the lifts and mechanical wizardry of the sport seem pitted against you. Parallel skiing is taught from the beginning, by-passing the embarrassing stem Christie as early as possible in your skiing career.

On the minus side, many French will not speak English, so we actually have to try and speak French. This is particularly the case with children's ski schools even if advertised as 'English speaking'. Resorts are less well organized than Switzerland and Austria. French hotels tend to be more expensive than Swiss/Austrian of a similar category, and service is rather less good. But French cuisine is as good as ever, particularly compared with some of its neighbours' blander offerings.

The notorious traffic jams between Moutiers and Val D'Isère, Tignes, Les Arcs, La Plagne and the Trois Vallées can be avoided by travelling on Sundays, but hotels are less co-operative about Sunday bookings. New roads are being built for the Savoie Olympics in 1992.

In conclusion, France is recommended for 'gastronomy on skis'.

Val Thorens is the highest resort in France, with sunny, year-round skiing for committed skiers in the Trois Vallées complex – one of the most exciting ski areas of the world. If you want to ski hard, this is the purpose-built resort for you.

Chamonix is a traditional Alpine village, now somewhat overgrown to accommodate a thriving summer and winter tourist industry. Villages are linked by the Mont Blanc ski pass. Les Houches is ideal for beginners, Argentière is hard and high. Ski the 'Vallée Blanche', off-piste from the Aiguille de Midi – a scenic wonder not to be missed.

Les Arcs is the home of ski évolutif. Catch the skiing bug for life here. Every facility is available in these three monolithic ski playgrounds. The Trois Vallées is a huge ski area for all standards. Les Arcs consists of three traffic-free ultra-modern purpose-built units, at 1600, 1800 and 2000, interconnected by lifts.
Arc Pierre Blanche (1600 m/5250 ft): being wood-faced this village is the most attractive of the three, combining a more homely atmosphere with the advantages of a modern resort. Ski lifts radiate from the centre and you can virtually ski to your front door.
Arc Chantel (1800 m/5900 ft): more modern-looking than 1600, split into two villages, Le Charvet and Les Villards. Ski school and children's facilities are particularly recommended.

Arc 2000 (2000 m/6500 ft): the newest and highest satellite in Les Arcs with access to some of the best, albeit least attractive skiing. Facilities include shops, boutiques, drugstore, games room, restaurants, night club, kindergarten, currency exchange, doctor, chemist, and covered car park.

Many north-facing slopes retain good snow. Les Arcs pass allows one day a week skiing at Tignes, Val D'Isère and La Plagne. Queuing is rarely a problem. The resort is lacking in social après-ski and bonhomie. Les Arcs may be quite smart when the French are there, when it is also busy, but in low season it is perhaps rather too popular with the British. Access is poor to tedious, not much for the non-skier.

SKIING IN THE ITALIAN ALPS

Skiing in the pasta Alps can be a lot of fun. It is generally sunnier on the southern, Italian side of the Alps, but this is offset by the fact that snowfall is less reliable in Italy and what snow

there is melts quicker. As a generalization the skiing season is shorter than its Alpine neighbours, particularly in a year of snow drought.

Arguably the Italians are less efficient than their northern neighbours, but they are extremely friendly and really do know how to enjoy a ski holiday and make you enjoy it too. *Après ski* is lively. Added to this is the excellence of Italian wine and food which make Italy, in a good snow year, hard to beat.

The main Alpine skiing areas are Piedmont (The 'Milky Way', with Sauze D'Oulx, Sestrière and Bardonecchia), the Aosta valley (Cervinia and Courmayeur), and the Dolomites (Cortina D'Ampezzo, Madonna de Campiglio, Val Gardena).

Skiing in the Italian Dolomites is unique for the beauty of the mountain scenery and because of the Dolomiti lift pass system, which is one of the most up-to-date and comprehensive in Europe, if not the world. The Superski Dolomiti lift pass covers over 450 resorts, which is ideal for the skier who likes to travel around and experiment with different resorts.

Courmayeur is to be found just through the Mont Blanc tunnel from Chamonix in France. This once-Roman spa favours those who prefer hotels rather than apartments. It is a friendly civilized resort with a wide variety of restaurants as well as activities for non-skiing members of the family.

One disadvantage is that it is not possible to ski back to the village, but otherwise there are good slopes for medium to advanced skiers in the main areas of Chécrouit, Arp and Val Veny. Another cable car goes from neighbouring Entrèves to the Monte Chétif, with terrific close-up views of the Monte Bianco massif. In a good year there is plenty of snow and facilities for cross-country skiing in Courmayeur.

Cervinia is one of the highest Alpine resorts, with one of the longest Italian seasons and best snow records. South-facing slopes with wide long runs abound. An additional bonus to this average-looking resort is the magnificent views of the Matterhorn (Monte Cervin). Zermatt in Switzerland is easily accessible for a day's skiing excursion. There is plenty of skiing for all standards except perhaps the very advanced. Main skiing areas are the high and often windy Plateau Rosa at 3480 m (11,417 ft), the Fruggen, the Plan Maison and the Carosello. It is extremely popular with the Italians and therefore very lively.

Cortina D'Ampezzo is the upmarket Italian resort, the Italian equivalent of St Moritz, Gstaad, and Lech rolled into one. In the heart of the Dolomites, Cortina is chic and fur-coated, with much for the non-skier too. It is one of the nicest larger resorts with a good choice of accommodation, particularly hotels, in the upper price range.

The main ski areas are the Faloria–Tondi area, accessible by cableway from the town centre, with open medium-grade runs; the Cristallo area, 6 km (4 miles) from the town centre with a bottom station at the foot of the Tre Croci pass and spectacular views of Dolomite rock from the top; the Tofana, with a tough top section of the run; and the Pocol, with gentle interconnecting runs.

SKIING IN THE GERMAN ALPS

Although not very well known among the British, Germany has some surprisingly good skiing in its Alpine regions. Resorts are attractive in true Alpine style, but tend to become rather busy with locals on weekends, when the snow is good. In the week they can be excellent and uncrowded.

Garmisch Partenkirchen is one of the best-known ski resorts, with its history of hosting the 1936 Winter Olympics, the 1978 World Championships and more recent World Cup downhill events.

56. *At the Königsee, Berchtesgaden.*

Over 50 cable cars and a train lead to a variety of ski areas, which contain two of Germany's highest mountains, the Alpspitze and the Zugspitze (2966 m/9731 ft), in the Wetterstein range; 110 km (70 miles) of Alpine skiing and 140 km (90 miles) of cross-country skiing is available. The main ski areas are the compact Eckbauergebiet; the Husberg/Kruzeck gebiet (which handles the majority of skiers); the Ostfeldergebiet (with bracing views and good albeit fairly short runs); the new and well-organized Wankgebiet; and the Zugspitze, which is reached in an hour by railway from the city centre. Skiing on the Zugspitze is below the summit of the Schneefernerhaus, with a long season helped by the glacier.

Berchtesgaden has much to offer the skier and non-skier for a winter holiday. The 'Berchtesgadener Land' is a conglomerate of attractive villages where tourist development has been tastefully controlled. This beautiful area is dominated by the Watzmann peaks. Additional attractions are cross-country skiing on the frozen lake Königsee with the pretty St Bartholemae church, a trip to the salt mines, the ice caverns and lively nightlife, and a natural ice bob sleigh run.

The Jenner ski area is suitable for the good intermediate skier, while the Rossfeld 'ski ohne grenze' runs over into Austria, with a new ski circus with skiing for all standards. The longest run here is 6 km (4 miles). The Hochschwarzeck has skiing for beginners and intermediates, while the Götschen is good for giant slalomers and motorway specialists. Cross-country skiing is also well served in the area with 55 km (35 miles) of prepared trails through the woods.

SKIING IN THE YUGOSLAV ALPS

It is only since the 1984 Sarajevo Winter Olympics that Yugoslavia has arrived on the international ski map. The main Alpine skiing in Yugoslavia is in Slovenia.

The best known resort is Kranjska Gora, host to FIS international slalom and giant slalom courses for over 20 years. Despite a relatively low altitude (800–1700 m/2500–5500 ft) it has good snow conditions on north-facing slopes, good motorway access and the oldest ski school in Slovenia.

Slopes are best suited to beginners, wide open and perhaps not too challenging for advanced skiers; 40 km (25 miles) of cross-country skiing is available. The nightlife is cheap and quite good fun, but not sophisticated by general Alpine standards.

The pretty lakeside town of Bled is also a good base for skiers in this area, although it does not have its own slopes. With curling and skating on the frozen lake, a tranquil spa-town atmosphere, it is well suited to families who like to mix tourism and skiing and travel independently to the slopes at Zatrnik or Pokljuka.

Bohinj also has a beautiful lake, with stunning views of the impressive Triglav, Yugoslavia's highest peak. Main skiing is on the Vogel plateau, with a good north-facing snow record. It can be cold in early season.

SELECTED SKI OPERATORS

Kuoni, Tel (071) 499 8636, have an extensive programme in Switzerland, including the charming Engadine valley and the Bernese Oberland.

Ski Thompson, Tel (071) 435 8431, have a huge brochure with packages in every Alpine country and some more besides.

Bladon Lines, Tel (081) 785 3131, have a large selection of chalets, hotels and self-catering apartments in France, Italy, Switzerland and Austria. Individually tailored holidays are available from the 'à la carte' department.

Made to Measure Holidays, Tel (0243) 533333, offer a 'one-stop travel shop' for all your skiing needs, whether you are looking for a low budget skiing package or a holiday to fit your own very specialized requirements. Personal service and detailed knowledge of resorts and hotels is their trademark.

Powder Byrne, Tel (071) 223 0601, specialize in 'real skiing' in Flims-Laax, St Moritz, Grindelwald and other up-market resorts. Much of the skiing is in search of powder with mountain guide Ueli Frei and royal guide Bruno Sprecher.

CHAPTER FOURTEEN

Mountain Dangers

Climb if you will, but remember that courage and strength are naught without prudence, and that momentary negligence may destroy the happiness of a lifetime. Do nothing in haste, look well to each step, and from the beginning think what may be the end.
— Whymper.

AVALANCHES

Press reports on avalanches over the last few years have been sensational and in many cases inaccurate, especially when the victims are well known. The uninformed reader might think that avalanches are the invention of the twentieth century and that skiing, or even just being present in a ski resort, has become unacceptably dangerous. Generally, this is not the case. Although more skiers than ever are skiing off piste in the avalanche danger zone, the sport as a whole is safer than it has ever been. Increased public awareness of the avalanche enigma will make it safer still.

The ideal season is when the first snows are preceded by low temperatures. A season with regular light snowfalls is preferable to a season when periods of heavy snowfall are mixed with weeks of snow-drought and sudden temperature changes. In a season where the danger remains high for a long time people are far more careful than when they think that the danger is confined to one short period or dangerous area.

The European press is less surprised than the British by avalanche accidents. Four people were killed in March 1988 by an avalanche in St Moritz, but with comparatively little media interest.

According to figures from the Weissfluhjoch (the Swiss avalanche institute), an average winter will claim some 160 lives in the main ski countries – France, Austria, Switzerland and Italy. About 120 of these will be off-piste skiers and mountaineers.

In fact local avalanche prediction, road closures, piste detonation and control in the Alps can deal with the majority of conditions to be expected in most winters. What cannot be prevented are sudden and violent temperature changes.

In the USA an average season might produce 10 to 15 fatalities. Avalanches are not seen statistically as a major threat to the recreational skier. This is largely attributable to the fact that skiing in the USA takes place in a very different atmosphere than in Europe. The active discouragement of off-piste skiing in the USA can be seen as a life-saver since wherever they occur, off-piste skiers in most cases start the avalanche which catches them.

American ski-runs are carefully managed. Dangers (and sources of litigation) are removed

wherever possible. Lift passes may be confiscated from those who disregard warnings. If a disobedient skier in the USA could be proven to have triggered an avalanche resulting in injury to another person, he would have little defence against the inevitable award of damages. American ski resort owners consider off-piste skiing in Europe as the sport of lunatics and express surprise that there are not even more accidents than at present.

The most satisfactory answer would seem to be to allow skiers the freedom of the mountains but to increase general avalanche awareness and avoidance.

Avalanches were not invented last ski season. They have been terrifying mountain people since time immemorial. Spontaneous natural avalanche triggers do occur, but in most cases known recurring avalanche tracks are protected by fences and plantations. Today the majority of accidents are triggered by skiers who have little or no knowledge of the avalanche risk.

57. Crossing avalanche debris.

Modern transport can take you from your office to the danger zone in a matter of hours with no more than your cheque book as a qualification for being in the mountains. Many assume that a ski resort is no more dangerous than a sloping beach.

Avalanche awareness

People are caught in avalanches because they disregard local warnings. They think that wearing an avalanche transceiver is a deterrent to the laws of nature. They ski on closed runs, through avalanche fences and young plantations which are there for protection.

If you limit your skiing to *the piste* in resorts you are statistically far safer than in normal life back home. But *off-piste*, a different set of rules applies, even in sight of the resort. Off-piste you are really in the mountains and must behave accordingly.

Two main types of avalanche occur – the loose snow and the slab avalanche. Loose snow avalanches can be wet snow or dry (powder, even airborne snow). Slabs are formed when snow is blown by wind onto lee slopes, breaking into blocks if the slope avalanches.

Particularly dangerous places include gullies, slopes with uncut grass beneath (get local information) and any route which traverses beneath a cornice. Cornices can fall and trigger an avalanche at any time.

In the Alps the majority of avalanche accidents occur on north and east facing lee slopes with a gradient of between 28 and 45 degrees. You can test the gradient of the slope with your ski sticks. You would be surprised how shallow a ski slope is, despite the speed you can ski. Lee slopes contain the best powder snow and so attract the most skiers. They are also the most dangerous since they often contain 'wind slab'. A skier anywhere on a wind slab can trigger a slope.

Comparatively safe places include thick forests, ridges, ground with big boulders, undulating ground if not too steep above.

Avalanches occur most frequently after heavy snow, especially if the snowfall is accompanied by wind, after rapid thaws, and in the afternoon on sunny slopes. Aim to be back on the piste before you begin to break through crusted snow.

Before leaving the piste, check local weather and avalanche forecasts. Ideally there should be no less than six in your off-piste party, equipped with avalanche transceivers and Recco radar reflectors. Practise until you are thoroughly familiar with using transceivers. Would you know how to summon emergency services? Allow plenty of time for your off-piste venture and budget your time with the weakest skier in mind.

Avoid suspect slopes at all costs, but if you have

58. Swiss rescue helicopter.

no alternative but to cross a potentially dangerous slope, warn all party members that it is dangerous, do up all clothing and re-check that transceivers are switched on, space out with a minimum of 50 m or yds between skiers, remove hands from ski stick loops.

Survival

Snow can weigh over half a ton per cubic yard. Death can easily occur from suffocation within minutes of burial under the snow. Do not assume that people who die in avalanches are unlucky. On the contrary, any survivor is extremely lucky.

However, if you are avalanched you can increase your chances as follows. Shout to the others the moment a slope starts to go. Decide the quickest route to safe terrain. Try to stay on your feet, skiing at 45 degrees to the fall-line. If you are caught, jettison your skis. Start to roll, rather than swim, away from the avalanche path. Keep trying to roll until the avalanche stops.

Witness and search

Mark the point where the skier was last seen. Search 'downstream' of this. Look around for other parties in the area who can help search. Appoint a leader. After half an hour, or sooner if people can be spared, send two people for outside help, with a written note of the time and place of the accident and the number of victims. Keep searching until a search party arrives, which may be a long time.

First aid

Clear head and chest so victim can breathe. Clear mouth and throat. Give artificial respiration if necessary. Keep victim warm and dry.

In conclusion

Only ski *off-piste* with someone who is an expert in local conditions. In most cases the only people with sufficient knowledge will be local mountain guides and ski instructors. Beware of the 'ski guides' offered by an increasing number of UK holiday companies. While some may have adequate avalanche awareness, the majority are not sufficiently qualified to lead off-piste parties. Insist on a qualified mountain guide or ski instructor.

On piste, you can ski without concern of the avalanche risk. Resorts will take every reasonable precaution to ensure your safety.

ALTITUDE SICKNESS

Whereas altitude problems in the Himalayas are obvious and people tend to take precautions, in the Alps many assume altitude is not important. In fact the majority of cases of altitude-related problems occur in the 2500 m (8000 ft) to 5000 m (16,000 ft) range, simply because in the Alps cable cars make such altitudes so accessible. Mont Blanc, highest summit in the Alps, is 4807 m (15,771 ft). Mechanical transport in the Alps will take you to the top of the Jungfraujoch (3454 m/11,332 ft) and the Aiguille du Midi téléférique (3842 m/12,605 ft). Many Alpine villages are in the 1000–2000 m (3300–6500 ft) range.

At 2000 m (6500 ft) most people will already be aware of the altitude if walking uphill. Above 2500 m (8200 ft), the loose rule is one day for every 300 m (1000 ft) of ascent. Without this, discomfort can turn into danger. Many mountaineers have great difficulty in sleeping above 2500 m (8200 ft) until acclimatized. You can be totally exhausted yet unable to sleep. Pace yourself very carefully before you have acclimatized. Sleeping pills may help.

Maximum acclimatization occurs after about three weeks, probably longer than your holiday. If you are travelling by car, ascending by téléférique and not exerting yourself or sleeping at altitude, the problem will be negligible. But if you intend to climb or ski mountaineer above 2500 m (8200 ft), a few days of gentle acclimatization in the 2500–3500 m (8200–11,500 ft) range will help greatly. 'Climb high, sleep low,' runs the mountaineers' motto.

People differ vastly in their ability to adapt to altitude. Strangely, acclimatization bears no relation to fitness. Indeed there is evidence that endurance-trained people, e.g. marathon runners, are actually less well able to acclimatize to altitude than others.

Sudden ascents to above 3500 m (11,500 ft) for the unacclimatized can be serious. Anyone suffering badly from altitude should descend for immediate relief. An altimeter is a useful tool not only to tell the altitude, but also as a barometer for weather and a navigational aid in cloud or fog. If it reads 4807 m (15,771 ft) you are either in a plane or on the summit of Mont Blanc.

THE EYE OF THE WIND

When the wind blows in the mountains, it changes the face of Mother Nature. At altitude, there is almost never a snow fall without wind. This will either be the prevailing wind or localized winds which are funnelled by valleys, passes and natural features. Wind from any direction is a danger signal in the high mountains – it is the builder of avalanches and cornices as well as causing wind chill to poorly protected skin.

If new snowfall is accompanied by wind, snow drifts can be disproportionately deeper than the

level of snowfall would suggest; 20 cm (8 in) of wind-blown snow (not in itself dangerous) could cause a drift 1 m (3 ft) deep (extremely dangerous). Drifted snow is dangerous not merely because of its depth, but because wind-driven snow forms a compacted layer called windslab which is dumped on lee slopes. Windslab is one of the most common causes of avalanche accidents and the least understood.

Cornices are formed by the wind. They resemble a frozen wave crest on the top of ridges, leaning out over the ridge in the leeward

59. *Aiguille du Midi.*

direction. The only thing which holds them in place is the tension in the wind-packed snow. The longer they stand, the more dangerous they become.

The wind chill factor is another nasty which is associated with wind. It is a subjective rather than an objective problem, being mainly relevant to exposed or badly insulated skin.

Here are some sample figures:

	Wind speed	5 mph (8 kph)	20 mph (30 kph)	30 mph (50 kph)	50 mph (80 kph)
Temp (°C) 0	Wind chill	−4	−14	−18	−20
−8		−13	−25	−31	−33
−16		−22	−37	−43	−46
−24		−31	−48	−56	−59

So when you are in the eye of the wind, remember the implications: increased avalanche danger, windslab and cornice formation, and the wind chill factor. To sum up: when it is windy in the Alps, wrap up well and keep off the snow unless you know what you are doing or are in a safe ski resort.

HYPOTHERMIA

Skiers, climbers and walkers who are inadequately dressed and are exposed to cold, wet or wind for sustained periods can quickly become victims of hypothermia. For years mountain hypothermia has been loosely known as exposure, but exposure to the elements is only part of its causes. Exposure causes rapid heat loss from the body, leading to a progressive fall of body temperature. Particularly dangerous is the combination of this factor with fatigue, cold, anxiety

60. Heavy weather.

and mental stress.

In mountain pursuits, the body is kept warm by a layer of still air next to the skin and between garments. When clothes become wet because of bad insulation or excessive sweating, water replaces the essential layer of air, reducing protection by up to 90 per cent. When this is exacerbated by windy conditions, further evaporation takes place which results in even greater cooling of the body.

It is the temperature of the core of the body (head, chest, stomach) which must be maintained to avoid danger from hypothermia. Once the core temperature falls 6°C or more below normal, the body starts to shiver in a late attempt to create heat by involuntary muscular activity.

Prevention of any mountain hazard is obviously better than cure. Proper mountain clothing is the first line of defence. 'Off the peg' ski suits may be fine for skiing in and around the resorts. But if you are skiing well away from the piste or touring you could get caught out by the weather. Then you will need real mountain clothing which still keeps you warm if it is wet or windy. In addition, sensible planning of the route according to the experience, fitness and skiing ability of the off-piste party will keep morale high and danger at a minimum.

The great danger of hypothermia is that it can be hard to spot. Some of the symptoms include apathy, pallor, disinterest, slow thinking, and inability to perform simple tasks well within the normal capability of the person concerned. Unexpected behaviour is another indication – unreasonable violent outbursts, slurred speech, stumbling, careless footwork, shivering and finally loss of consciousness. By no means can all of these symptons be expected to manifest themselves at the same time.

In the mountains, insulation and removal of the causes are the required immediate treatment. Early recognition should be followed by re-allocation of loads, change of direction to downhill or downwind, extra clothing, body warming by getting into a huddle, seeking shelter from the wind, warming with hot drinks and energy-giving food. The next step is for the party leader to organize a safe and quick evacuation to a place where a serious case can be actively re-warmed. Remember that once the onset of hypothermia has begun, it is already too late for the sufferer to reason clearly enough to get himself out of trouble. It is the rest of the party who must now do this for him.

For further information, contact the British Mountaineering Council.

SNOW-BLINDNESS

Freshly fallen snow reflects up to 90 per cent of sunlight. Solar radiation can be up to four times as strong above 2000 m (6500 ft) than at sea level. Ultraviolet radiation is absorbed by the surface of the eye in the same way as it is absorbed by the skin. The only difference is that the surface of the eye cannot get a tan and develop its own protection. We need to do what nature cannot – and use adequate sunglasses.

Sunburn of the eye tissues results in snow-blindness. During the period of exposure only the brightness of the light serves as a warning. Snow-blindness develops some eight to ten hours later. Frequently, skiing sunglasses are seen as just another fashion asset, but for the off-piste skier and ski mountaineer who puts in long hours on the snow, light absorbency and side-protection, rather than fashion, should be the main criteria. Glasses need to absorb over 80 per cent of the light to provide adequate protection. Special mountaineers' glasses are available which fit snugly round the sides of the eye and offer maximum protection.

At really high altitude, goggles may be safer. Do not forget to apply sunscreen to the eyelids to prevent burning. Always carry a spare pair of glasses if going on a tour. In an emergency, lenses can be made out of cardboard with a thin slit to see through – unfashionable, but quite effective. You should not assume that overcast days are any less dangerous – ultraviolet light penetrates just as effectively through cloud.

The first sign of snow-blindness is a dry irritation of the eye, perhaps a flickering in front of the eyes followed by a burning sensation and finally a feeling as if the eyes are full of sand. Blinking and exposure to any light source can be extremely painful. Confinement to a darkened room for a few days with cold compresses is often the best remedy for acute cases – punishment indeed for a few hours of carelessness. But happily in most cases the eyes heal spontaneously and there are no lasting effects.

So if you forget or lose your sunglasses, don't be tempted to squint onwards for the rest of the day – especially if you plan to go on a day tour involving long stretches on a glacier at high altitude. Snow-blindness can ruin the 'après' as well as the 'ski'.

CREVASSE RESCUE

Crevasses on glaciers are a major danger for off-piste skiers and mountaineers, yet all too often the danger is only considered when a rescue becomes necessary. Crevasse rescue drill should be practised by any group long before reaching the glacier. Currently there are a wide variety of methods used and every guide will have his favourite. For the moment, be sure each party member knows which method would be used, and practises it until it becomes second nature.

The risk is not just confined to high-altitude ski tourers or mountaineers. Many ski lifts give access to off-piste glacier runs for skiers who have no idea of the danger from below. Guides are often horrified to see parties gulping wine and giggling over their lunchtime picnic, quite oblivious to the softening snow bridge on which they have decided to rest.

Always wear a full body harness on glacial terrain. Travelling uphill or on the flat, the party should be roped together. The problems of skiing downhill roped to others often outweigh the advantages. If you fall in when skiing down, you just have to rely on the others to pull you out. Always wear ski safety straps on glaciers, or you may lose a ski down a crevasse on top of your other problems.

Those who fall into a crevasse often only go waist deep. Others who disappear from sight do not, as you might think, drop into a void. They can be jammed against the sides or find themselves a few feet down on a ledge or snow bridge. Extraction problems can be extreme if a victim is unconscious or, as often happens, body heat melts the side of the crevasse which then refreezes and cements him to the side. The frictional forces involved usually mean setting up pulley systems, which increase rescuers' traction by a factor of ten or even twelve.

61. Happy is the man with the right snow glasses.

CHAPTER FIFTEEN

More Alpine Sports

Great things are done when men and mountains meet,
This is not done by jostling in the street.
— Blake.

Alpine recreation is by no means confined to skiing, walking and climbing. In every area, the locals have got the process of enjoying the great outdoors down to a fine art. Here is a selection of more unusual Alpine adventures, some dangerous, some tranquil, some of which will appeal only to the cheque-book adventurer who is prepared to pay for a thrill in the air, on the water, on two wheels, four legs, perhaps even at 130 kph (80 mph) on ice or snow.

Hang-gliding

The serious participant would do well to take lessons at home before leaving for the Alps, but for those who just want to buy the thrill, it is possible to take a tandem ride in the company of an expert. On skis in winter, on foot in summer, a téléférique will take you to an Alpine peak and after some rudimentary instruction, signing cheques and disclaimers, off you go into the void. A tandem ride in the company of an experienced pilot is undoubtedly the best way to sort out your motivation and decide whether you would like to train for solo flight. Many Alpine centres have these 'tourist rides'. Despite the comparative novelty of the sport, it is already too late to be the first to descend from most well known Alpine peaks. In France, Christophe Vaillant has already

jumped off the summit of Mont Blanc and the Grandes Jorasses strapped to his 'delta wing'!

Parapente

Parapente too is a newcomer to the Alps, a form of steerable parachute. James Bond was not unique in using it to great notoriety in his speedy retreat from the Schilthorn, when under some pressure to get home for the *après ski*. On a clear day in the Chamonix valley, the sky is dotted with hang-gliders and parapentes making dramatic arrivals in the village. From a distance it looks easy. But the vagaries of localized winds and turbulence make this a sport only for the trained. As with most aerial sports, problems only arise when you hit the ground. Again some familiarization before leaving home is advised, although 'tandem' rides are available in the company of an experienced pilot. In the Alps, courses lasting a week will cost from £100 upwards. Many well-known Alpinists have used the parapente as a quick way to get home after climbing a major peak. The parapente folds into a neat medium-sized backpack.

Gliding

A good place to watch and participate in gliding is in the Engadine valley, based on the airport at

62. *Balloons, Château D'Oex.*

Samedan. In appropriate conditions, gliders make a fantastic spectacle against the mountain backdrop when viewed from the restaurant at the top of the Muottas Muragl railway.

Ballooning in the Alps

In 1783 the Montgolfier brothers, while sitting by the fire, observed the lifting power of warm air and the idea of ballooning was born. The first pioneers were a sheep, a cock and a duck, but modern passenger balloons carry four to six passengers and a professional pilot.

One of the major Alpine ballooning events is held annually in Château D'Oex, Canton Vaud, Switzerland, in the month of January. More than 60 balloons representing 20 countries take part each year. Château D'Oex is unique in the world of ballooning in that the local valley winds are 'steerable'. Winds travelling different directions criss-cross the valley at different altitudes.

Experienced local pilots know where these winds will be on a given day and can travel up down and across the valley with surprising accuracy.

Winter is the best season for ballooning in the Alps since there is less turbulence because of less hot air. Even if it is quite windy it is not cold, because when you are airborne you travel at the same speed as the wind, so you do not feel it. This, you may think, is a most novel way to avoid the wind chill factor.

A hot air balloon folds up into a one-metre cube of material, which with the basket will fit onto a car trailer. Inflated, it stands 25 m (80 ft) high and can carry seven people to an altitude of 4000 m (13,000 ft). During the ballooning week, international teams play 'hare and hounds' or enter distance and navigational competitions as well as target challenges set by local cheeseries and hotels. Other remarkable sights which can be seen are miniature radio-controlled balloons, as well as numerous weird balloons designed for advertising – a Sphinx, a floating bottle of washing-up liquid, a Zeppelin, a flying Swatch, to name but a few.

Members of the public are welcome to join in the festival. One hour's flight will cost in the region of £100, but for this unique way of seeing the Alps it is well worth it. For further details contact the tourist office of Château D'Oex, CH 1837, tel (029) 4 77 88.

River rafting in the Alps

One is not always aware of Alpine rivers, so often are they hidden by deep gorges or seen from above, seemingly inaccessible on railway journeys. But many Alpine rivers provide exciting opportunities for river rafting and kayaking.

Rafting is done in inflatable rafts, with four to six passengers, one or two professionals on board. Safety helmets, waterproofs and life jackets are worn. The rafts are some 4 m (13 ft) long, about 2 m (6ft 6 in) wide. Accidents are rare, and the experience is exhilarating to say the least.

In France, suitable rivers in the northern Alps are the Doron, Arve, Isère; in the southern Alps, the Durance, Ubaye, Drac, Verdon and Haut-Var. In France, contact the Rafting and Kayak Federation for further information at 17, route de Vienne, 69007 Lyon, tel 72 73 43 00.

In Switzerland, the Eurotrek Wild Water School runs beginners' courses and advanced river-running trips. Venues include the Engadine (River Inn), the Bernese Oberland (the Aare, Simme, Saane), through Switzerland's Grand Canyon (the Rhein gorge) with canoe trips, as well as a wild-water school. Contact Eurotrek at Corviglia Tennis Center, Postfach 68, 7500 St Moritz Bad, CH, tel (082) 31500. For day tours through the Rhein gorge contact Swissraft on (086) 34141.

Rafting is also possible on the Dorea Baltea (Italy).

Windsurfing is popular in the summer on all Alpine lakes.

For a more relaxing holiday a vast choice of Alpine spas provide fresh air and curative waters. Spas were one of the most popular holiday locations in the Alps for curing all sorts of aches and pains, and still attract many visitors who just want to get away from it all in spirit-lifting scenery.

Bikes and mountain bikes

Bicycles can be hired in many railway stations across the Alps. In Austria, the rates are from as little as 35 AS per day. A detailed Austrian cycling map is available from the tourist office. In Switzerland many stations have hire facilities which enable you to return a bicycle to another station without extra charge. This makes it possible to plan routes where a train is taken to a high pass, dismount with your bike and spend a leisurely half day on a downhill-only tour. Route maps are available from Swiss stations.

For the more adventurous, a cycle tour of the Alps may be just the ticket, although this may be arduous due to the great differences in altitude in even short tours. France and Italy are two nations of bicycle lovers. In France I have found motorists unusually considerate to the cyclist, even on busy roads. If someone cuts in too sharply it is probably not a Frenchman.

Off the beaten track mountain bikes are great favourites, but have only been seen in the Alps in the last ten years, originating, like so many new waves, in California. These light, strong and multi-geared bikes will not be found at railway stations but are hired in specialist Alpine centres.

They can be hired as easily as a pair of skis, ridden as easily as an ordinary bike, but test the brakes when you first get on them or you may find yourself pitched over the handlebars. Remember only to ride where permitted (some

paths are banned to bikers). Remember also that the versatility of these bikes can place you away from help in the mountains far more quickly than walking, so aim at being self-sufficient in terms of map reading and mountain safety.

Riding in the Alps

An increasingly popular way to take in the view, day or week long riding safaris are available in most parts of the Alps. In Switzerland, Davos has riding courses, trekking is available in central and eastern Switzerland, including hiking with horse-drawn waggons and gypsy safaris. You can travel on ancient mule-tracks through the Oberhasli Valley and the Jungfrau region or the Valais. In winter, tourists may like to watch the unusual sport of ski-jöring at St Moritz, where skiers are pulled by horses at high speeds on the frozen lake. In France, contact the A.N.T.E., 15 rue de Bruxelles, 75009 Paris, tel 42 81 42 82, for

63. The Alps by bike.

general information about riding tours.

In Austria, there is a wide choice of trekking ponies, including the famous Haflinger. Specialist riding trips lasting several days are available in the Vorarlberg, staying in Alpine guesthouses and mountain refuges. The Tirol has some 70 riding stables with horses to suit every standard. In Styria the great attraction is the famous Lippizaner horse farm at Piber near Graz.

The Alps at 130 kph (80 mph) – The Cresta Run

Described by Clement Freud as 'the ultimate laxative' the Cresta Run opens in January and February at St Moritz in Switzerland's Engadine. Although it is a private British-run club, members of the public are able to participate, under strict direction, as members of the 'supple-

mentary list' to ride the run when the members list has finished for the morning.

The Cresta Run (rebuilt every year) has just celebrated its centenary. During this period the 1200 m (4000 ft) ice toboggan run record has been halved from 100 to 50 seconds. Elite riders can reach in excess of 130 kph (80 mph) riding from 'Top', but beginners start from 'Junction' and their speed is considerably less. Helmet, goggles, knee and elbow pads and spiked shoes make you resemble the unfortunate offspring of

64. *On the Cresta Run.*

a gladiator and a motorcycle policeman as your name is called to the box and you lie on the 'skeleton', the correct name for the sledge. Supplementary list riders receive the loan of equipment, tuition and five rides in the season for around £110. It is not cheap, but it is certainly a thrill.

Also in St Moritz is the *four-man bob run.*

This is essentially a high speed tourist taxi ride, costing around £35. No skill is required here. Two tourists are sandwiched between an experienced driver and brake man, and gravity does the rest, forcing your head down into your anorak on the banked corners for a breathtaking ride.

65. *The four man bob.*

66. Crevasses on Mont Blanc.

Index

*(figures in italics denote b/w illustrations, those in **bold** the number of a colour plate)*